日本料理

むきものハンドブック

四季折々の料理を彩る野菜の飾り切り

島谷宗広 著

Handbook on Japanese Food:

Carving Techniques
for Seasonal Vegetables

MUNEHIRO SHIMATANI

誠文堂新光社

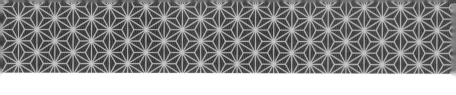

はじめに

日本料理をより魅力的に、より華やかに彩る「むきもの」は、
昔から年中行事や祭事の際に料理を引き立たせてきた名脇役です。

しかし調理の現場では、むきものはムダが多い上に手間がかかり、
そこに人員もかけられないことから敬遠される傾向にあります。
また、「料理との効果的な組み合わせが分からない」
との声も聞こえてきます。

そこで本書では、むきもの初心者にも分かりやすいよう
手順写真を多く掲載して丁寧に解説するとともに
料理例を示し、より実践的に紹介しています。

伝統の技は、決して古臭いものではありません。
料理のイメージとデザイン次第で、新しいものにもなり得るのです。
繰り返して「切れる」感覚を身につけ、
四季を存分に取り入れた料理を楽しんでください。

島谷　宗宏

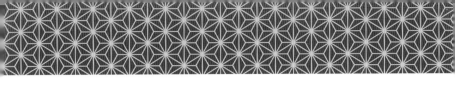

PREFACE

Food carving has always played an important role in Japanese cuisine
in order to enhance the presentation of food for seasonal events and
festivals.

However, at restaurant kitchens, cooks tend to avoid intricate procedures
to save time and avoid food waste. Also, we often hear cooks say "It's
hard to choose which techniques to use with which food."

In this book I am introducing practical carving art with as many step-by-
step photos as possible so that even a beginner will easily catch on.

Traditional techniques never become old-fashioned.
Your imagination and design can lead to brand-new culinary creations on
the plate.
Practice repeatedly until you acquire a true sense of "cutting," and enjoy
cooking by creatively incorporating the season into each presentation.

Munehiro Shimatani

◆ In this book you will find a technical term "mukimono." Mukimono stands for decoratively
peeled or carved vegetables.

目次

Contents

むきものの基本

むきものを始めるにあたって、
まずおさえておきたい基本のテクニックを紹介します。
土台となる最初の工程を丁寧で正確にむくことが、
美しいむきものへとつながります。

MUKIMONO BASICS

Here are very basic peeling/shaping techniques to begin with. Learning how to peel foods into basic shapes should be mastered first. If you can "peel" such basic shapes carefully and precisely, then you are half way to a beautiful result.

SHIKAKU

四角

<small>しかく</small>

Cubes

丸く木取った（切って形を作る）弧を切り落とし、ひとつの角を90°にして4辺の長さをそろえ、正四角柱を作ります。垂直に包丁を入れて4回で木取るのがベストですが、ズレがあれば微調整して整えましょう。

As most vegetables are round in shape, a square prism is made by cutting away circular edges vertically on all four sides making each corner 90°.
Check that each length is the same, and adjust by slicing off excess.

◆角を90°に、4辺の長さをそろえて木取る基本の四角です。
The basic cube, with 90° corners and equal length sides.

1

必要な長さに切り、皮をむいて丸く木取る。

Cut into required size and peel around into a cylinder.

2

まな板に寝かせて置き、まな板に対して垂直に包丁を入れ、弧を切り落とす。

Place on a cutting board round face down, and cut vertically against the surface, to remove a circular side.

3

2で切り落とした辺を下にしてまな板に置き、垂直に包丁を入れて2辺目を切り落とす。

Place cut side down, and cut vertically against the surface to remove the second circular side.

4

食材を回して切り落とした辺を下にし、垂直に包丁を入れて3辺目を切り落とす。1辺目と平行になるよう注意する。

Turn to remove the third side with vertical motion of your knife so that the cut side is parallel to the first side.

5

4と同様に4辺目も切り落とす。

Repeat with the remaining side.

6

4辺の長さがそろい、角が90°の正四角柱になっているか確認し、ズレがあれば微調整する。

Check that four sides have equal lengths and equal 90°corners. Slice off more, if necessary, to shape into a square prism.

包丁を垂直に入れて、すべての角を90°に切り落とす。4辺が同じ長さになるようにする。

Work knife vertically to make each corner at 90°, and each side equal in length.

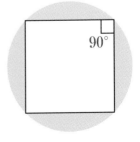

90°

HANGETSU
半月
はんげつ
Half-moons

丸く木取り、さらに半分に切った形を月の半分が輝いて
いる状態になぞらえて、半月と呼びます。複雑なむきも
のを作る場合にも、基礎となることが多く、丁寧にむき
たい形です。

A round slice split into half is called Half-moon as it
resembles the shining shape exactly. Cut this shape precisely
when you prepare it as a base for more intricate designs.

◆丸く木取ったものを半分にした形です。
Halved Round Shape

1

基本をおさえて丁寧に丸く木取り、ちょうど半分になるよう、垂直に包丁を入れて切る。

Choose a straight section of the vegetable and cut out a round that is evenly thick. Cut in half vertically.

2

切り口がシャープになっていることを確認する。

Check that the edges are sharply cut and right angled.

ICHO

いちょう
Gingko Leaves

丸から半月に木取り、さらに半分に切った形がいちょうの葉に見えることから、いちょうと呼びます。だいこんなどの大きなものから小さな形をむく場合や、煮物などでも用いられます。

Icho, or gingko nut leaf, is named after the fan-like shape of a quarter split of a round slice. Large sized vegetables such as daikon are cut into this smaller shape. This is also used for Nimono, or simmered vegetable.

◆丸、半月、いちょうと変化した形です。
Round slice is cut into equal quarters, into Icho.

1

基本をおさえて丁寧に半月に木取り、さらにちょうど半分になるよう、垂直に包丁を入れて切る。

Cut a round precisely into halves and then into quarters, carefully working the knife in a vertical motion.

2

切り口はシャープに、角は直角になっていることを確認する。

Check that the edges are sharply cut with right angled corners.

MARU MENTORI

丸面取り
Beveled Rounds

面取りは食材を料理に使う際に、切り口の角を薄くそぎ落とす下ごしらえです。主に根菜類を煮るときに行い、角から煮崩れするのを防ぎます。このひと手間で、料理の見栄えがよくなります。

Mentori is a beveling technique useful for retaining the cut shape of root vegetables while being cooked. Just adding this procedure to preparation makes a big difference in presenting the dish.

◆ **煮崩れを防ぐひと手間です。**
This simple procedure prevents breakage of the shape while being simmered.

1

切った食材の角を薄くそぎ落とし、尖った角をなくす。

Trim away corners of sharp cut edges to make smooth surfaces.

2

切り口がいくつかあるときには、すべての角を薄くそぎ落として面取りする。

Repeat along all cut edges, if any.

ROKKAKU
ろっ かく
六角
Hexagons

丸く木取った中に六角を木取っていきます。ひとつの角が120°になるよう、包
丁を入れて切り落とします。包丁は一息に引くことが、切り口をシャープに
整えるポイントです。

After cutting into a round block, trim the sides into 6 faces so that a hexagonal
column is formed. Cut away sides at six faces, leaving six 120° corners. To make
sharp corners it is important to draw the knife in a single motion without hesitation.

◆ 角を120°に、相対する辺を平行に木取る基本の六角です。
Basic hexagon is made with 120° corners and parallel opposite edges.

1

必要な長さに切り、皮をむいて丸く
木取る。

Cut out desired length and peel the
sides into a column.

2

六角形の1辺を切り落とす。包丁は
ためらうと切り口がガタガタしてし
まうので、一息に引く。

Slice off one side. Move the knife in
one smooth motion because hesitation
will cause rough surfaces.

3

角が120°になるように包丁の刃を
合わせる。

Apply edge of the knife at a position
to make 120º corner. Slice off the first
side in a single motion.

4

包丁を一息に引いて2辺目を切り
落とす。

Slice off the second side by drawing
the knife cleanly through.

5

4辺目は相対する辺と並行に、なお
かつ角が120°になるようにする。

Apply the knife parallel to the first cut
edge, at an angle of 120º on the corner.

6

5、6辺目も5と同様に相対する辺
と並行に、なおかつ角が120°になる
ように切り落とす。

Slice off in the same manner again and
make 5th and 6th faces.

ひとつの角を120°に、相対する辺が
平行になるようにする。丸の中をめ
いっぱい使って大きく木取る。

Be sure to cut opposite edges parallel
to each other, leaving 120º corners.
Slice off as little as possible inside
the circle.

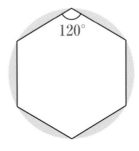

GOKAKU
五角
<ruby>五角<rt>ご かく</rt></ruby>

Pentagons

ひとつの角が108°のため、正五角形に木取るのは難しいものですが、何度も
練習して感覚をつかみましょう。まな板を利用すると切りやすくなります。

This shaping, with 5 angles of 108° each, is hard to acquire. Practice until
you get the right feeling. A cutting board will help you create sharply cut sides.

◆角を108°に、相対する辺の中心に角がくるように木取る基本の五角です。

Basic pentagon is made with 108° corners. Be sure that each corner is opposite the center of the flat side.

1

必要な長さに切り、皮をむいて丸く
木取る。

Cut out a length you need, and peel the
sides into a column.

2

まな板に寝かせて置き、まな板に対
して72°に包丁を入れる。5つの辺
の長さがすべて同じことを頭に入れ
ておく。

Place on a cutting board round face
down. Hold the knife at an angle of
72 ° against the board, and slice off
one side. Remember to cut the same
width at all 5 edges.

3

2で切り落とした辺を下にしてまな板に置き、同じ角度で包丁を入れて切り落とす。

Place on the cutting board sliced side down. Cut away another side moving the knife at the same angle.

4

2、3を繰り返して五角に木取る。

Repeat Steps 2 and 3 to form a pentagon.

5

角はすべて108°、辺は同じ長さ、相対する辺の中心に角がくるようにすると美しい形になる。

Check that each angle has 108° and all 5 sides are the same length. Remember that the corner point is positioned in the center of the opposite side.

ひとつの角は108°なので、まな板に対して72°の角度で包丁を入れて五角に木取る。

Pentagon has five 108° corners. Slice at an angle of 72° against the cutting board.

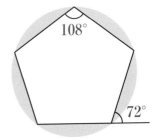

ROPPO

ろっぽう
六方
Rounded Hexagons

里いもやかぶなど、球形の野菜を丸みをそのまま生かしながら皮をむいていく
方法です。主に煮物に用い、見栄えがよく、煮崩れもしにくくなります。

Round shaped vegetables such as taro and turnip can be peeled into this shape,
bringing out the best of their natural features. Lovely to look at, this shape is mainly
used for Nimono, or simmered dishes, as it prevents breakage while being cooked.

◆断面は六角に、側面は丸みを持たせる 球形野菜の基本のむき方です。
Basic global peeling with hexagon ends and bulging sides.

1

上下を切り落とし、断面が平行にな
るようにする。

Cut away both ends so that the cut
edges are parallel.

2

六角に木取る要領で、断面が六角に
なるように包丁の刃を入れる。

Insert knife in the same manner as
ROKKAKU so that each end forms a
hexagon.

20

3

側面は野菜の丸みに合わせ、野菜に対して包丁の角度を一定にしてむく。

Peel along the round side, keeping the angle of knife fixed against the vegetable.

4

同様に断面の角が120°になるように6辺をむく。

Repeat to form six sides making 120° at each corner.

5

皮が同じ厚さでむけているかを右手の親指で感じながらむくと、包丁の角度が一定になる。

Try to guide the thickness of peeled skin with your thumb by feeling it. Always check that you peel an even thickness. This way your knife will stay at a fixed angle.

断面の形は六角と同様に、ひとつの角が120°で相対する辺が平行。側面は野菜の丸みをそのまま生かす。

Shape the flat ends in the same manner as ROKKAKU, keeping opposite sides parallel to each other, creating an angle of 120°.

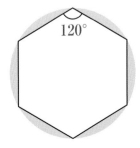

桂むき
(かつら)

Paper Thin Peeling

桂むきはむきものの基本であり、包丁づかいの基本でもあります。数をこなして練習を重ね、切れる感覚を体に覚え込ませましょう。スピードよりも、均一な厚さにむくことが大切です。

Katsura-muki is one of the very basic techniques of mukimono, and also of knife work.
You may need to try many times until you get the feeling of this technique. Pursue even thickness rather than the peeling speed.

◆包丁づかいの基本中の基本。厚さを均一にむいていきましょう。
The most basic of all knife skills; peeling an even thin strip of "paper."

1

できるだけ太くて真っすぐなだいこんを選び、葉を切り落とす。

Choose a thick and straight vegetable (daikon is used here). Cut away leafy section.

2

適当な長さに切る。長くなるほど難易度が上がる。これは20cmほど。

Cut into desired length. The longer the length, the harder the work. This block measures approx. 20cm. You may wish to begin with a shorter block.

3

皮を薄くむきながら、太さのそろった円柱になるよう、2周ほどむいて整える。

Peel the skin thinly, then continue to peel the inside around once more, at the same time shaping the column into even thickness.

4

上から下まで均一な太さに整った
状態。

Now an evenly thick column is ready.

5

右の親指は刃の上に置き、左の親指
は右よりやや上に置いて桂むきをす
る。

Put your right thumb on the knife
edge, your left thumb a little above,
and slowly work the knife to the left.

6

薄く厚さを均一にむく。厚さは用途
によって使い分ける。

Carefully peel as thinly and evenly as
possible, although the thickness you
choose depends on what the peel is
used for.

7

包丁は押して切るのではなく上下に
動かし、左手で野菜を回して切る。
左右の親指で薄さを感じながら切っ
ていく。

Do not push the knife. Move subtly up
and down, turning the vegetable with
your left hand. Check the thickness
by feeling with your right thumb as
you work.

8

むけなくなる細さまでつなげて桂む
きにする。

Continue peeling until the vegetable is
too thin to peel.

むきもので使う道具と
使い方のコツ
Mukimono Tools and Tricks

本書で使用したむきものの道具とその使い方のコツを紹介します。むき
もの専用の道具も多々ありますが、買いそろえなくても薄刃包丁があれ
ばむくことができます。使いやすい道具を選び、季節感のあるむきもの
や表情のあるむきもので、料理を引き立てる名脇役を生み出しましょう。

Mukimono utensils used for this book are introduced here, with the
recommended usage of them. You might find various specialized knives
made for mukimono, but I would recommend a single Usuba-bocho, or thin
bladed knife. Choose an easy-to-handle tool, and create the seasonal touch or
expressions for your dish.

USUBA-BOCHO
薄刃包丁
うすばほうちょう
Thin-bladed Knife

野菜切り専用の包丁。むきもののほと
んどはこれが1本あればむくことがで
きる。名前の通り、刃が薄く作られて
いる片刃の包丁。

Specially made to cut vegetables, an
usuba-bocho (pronounced hocho when
named alone) will go a long way. As the
name suggests, it is a thin knife with a
single blade.

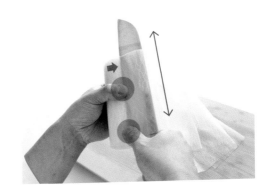

むく
Peeling

右の親指は刃と野菜が接しているところに、左の
親指は右よりやや上に置き、むいている薄さと包
丁の刃の角度を親指の腹で感じる。包丁は上下に
動かし、左手で野菜をゆっくり包丁側へ回しなが
らむく。

Position your right thumb where the blade touches
the vegetable, left thumb at a little higher position as
shown. Always feel the thickness and the angle of
knife with your thumbs. Move the knife up and down
gently with your right hand, at the same time turning
the vegetable towards the knife with your left hand.

切る
Cutting

包丁を垂直におろして切る。別の方向に包丁を入れるときにも、野菜を回して包丁は常に同じ位置で切る。

Insert the knife vertically to cut. Fix the knife position and turn the vegetable when cutting again.

刃先で切る
Cutting with Knife Tip

尖っている部分を利用すると、細かい作業がしやすい。より細かい作業をするときには、刃を立てて使う。

Use the pointed tip when doing intricate work. For more intricate carving, hold the knife upright.

刃全体で切る
Cutting with A Slicing Motion

刃元から切り始め、包丁を手前に引いて、刃先まで長さを最大限に使って切る。包丁を大きく動かして使う。

Using the bottom of the blade first, pull the knife towards you boldly to use the whole blade up to the tip.

刃元で切る
Cutting with Knife Base

深く切り込みを入れたいときに使う。右の親指を包丁から浮かし、どれくらいの深さまで入っているか確認する。

When making a deep score, insert the base of knife, checking the depth with your right thumb by detaching from the knife.

GYUTO
牛刀
ぎゅうとう
Cleaver

万能包丁とも呼ばれ、肉をはじめ野菜など
何にでも用いられる。反りが大きいため、か
ぼちゃなど硬い野菜を切り分けるのに便利
な両刃の包丁。

Also called "almighty knife," the cleaver is
widely used to cut meats or vegetables. It is
double-bladed (sharp on both faces) with more
curve than the usuba-bocho, making work such
as splitting a pumpkin, easy.

安定した場所に硬い野菜を置き、包丁
を入れて左手の母指球（親指の付け根の
ふくらみ）を刃先側に添えて、真っすぐ
体重をのせるようにして切る。

Place a hard vegetable on a stable
surface, and insert tip of the knife.
Putting your left thenar (the thick and soft
part under the thumb) on the knife tip, cut
vertically, keeping your body weight on
the knife.

TSUTSU-NUKI
筒抜き
Corer

丸く抜くときに用いる。さまざまなサイズが
あり、野菜の大きさや用途に応じて合うも
のを選ぶ。筒状の穴を開ける場合には、左
右に差し込んで取るときれいに仕上がる。

Japanese corers come in thinner fluted tubes
than Western apple corers. I choose the size
according to the vegetable size and purpose.
To make a tubular hole, insert corer from both
ends for a neat finish.

ペティナイフ
Petty Knife

刃先が鋭く、繊細な作業向き。本書では、桔梗きゅうりをむくのに使用した。

This small knife has a sharp tip that is suitable for delicate work. In this book I used this knife to make the Bell Flower Cucumber.

刃先が鋭く尖っているので、小さなものにも切れ目を入れやすい。野菜の大きさや作業の細かさに合わせて使い分ける。

The pointed tip is useful for making slits into small vegetables. Choose the size of knife according to the size of vegetables and carving work.

筒抜きの先が鋭いので、まな板の上で使用する場合には、傷つけないようにふきんなどを敷く。

Since the edge of tsutsu-niki is very sharp, lay a dish cloth over cutting board to protect the surface.

IMO-NUKI

いも抜き
Mellon Ballers

穴や丸い玉をくり抜くときに用いる。さま
ざまなサイズがあり、野菜の大きさや用途に
応じて合うものを選ぶ。本書では、六方小
かぶのくり抜きやキウイを玉にするのに使
用した。

Used to cut out holes or balls, mellon ballers
come in many sizes. Choose the right one for
the size of vegetable or fruit and the purpose.
I used this for Roppo Ko-kabu and kiwi balls.

野菜に対してかぶせるように当て、手
首を回転させて丸く抜き取る。

Apply baller to cover the food, and scoop
out the flesh by twisting your wrist.

SANKAKU NOMI

三角のみ
Corner Chisel

筋をつけるのに用いる。本書では、青葉冬
瓜やオレンジなどに使用した。

This chisel is used to make scores. I use this for
Aoba Togan and oranges.

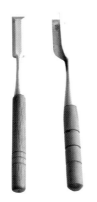

NOMI

のみ
Chisels

氷彫刻に用いる。冷し素麺七夕仕立の氷の
器を作るのにも使用する。

This is used for creating ice sculpture. I use one
to make a container for a summer dish.

溶けやすい氷の彫刻は、スピードと技
術が必要。また、滑りやすいので軍手
をし、破片でケガをしないためにも
ゴーグルを。

Ice sculpture requires speed and
techniques. Be sure to wear goggles to
protect your eyes and cotton gloves to
hold the slippery ice.

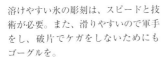

野菜に対して真っすぐに刃を当てて
削るように滑らす。力任せに動かすと、
割れの原因になるので注意。

Hold the chisel so the v-shaped blade
faces the vegetable straight on, and slide
as if you are shaving it. Do not push
heavily as it may split the whole shape.

野菜の特性を生かす
Make the Most of Each Vegetable

むきものは「切る」だけでなく、
野菜の特性を利用して形作ることが多くあります。
それぞれの野菜の特性を理解し、知っておくことが大切です。
まずは、基本中の基本をおさえましょう。

Mukimono is not only about cutting vegetables but taking advantage of each one.
Try to understand natural features. Here are simple basics.

◆皮を厚くむく野菜
Peeling Thickness

かぶ、うど、里いもなどは皮付近に筋があるため、皮を厚くむきます。では、どこまで厚くむけばいいか？ かぶなどには、輪切りにすると内側に輪があるのが分かります。このラインの内側までかなり厚くむくことで、口当たりがよくなります。

Vegetables such as kabu, taro, or udo have tough fibers under the skin, and need the thick peeling to remove them. But, how thick? Check the thickness of such fibers by slicing a piece before peeling off varying thicknesses. When you have removed the right amount, the mouth-feel is smooth.

かぶなどの厚くむいた皮は、捨てずに取っておいてきんぴらなどに。

Keep the thickly peeled skin for later use. Cut and add to soups, or use for stir-fried dishes.

◆繊維の方向を生かす
Use Direction of Fibers

むいた野菜を水にさらすと、繊維の力で切れ目が開いたり、繊維が引っ張られて巻くなど表情がつきます。形作ったそのままの状態をキープさせたいときには、氷水を使うこともあります。

Vegetable curls or bends can be made by cutting along the fibers before soaking in cold water. The fibers pull the cut sections apart or cause the curls to be more pronounced. In order to keep the curls, ice water is used sometimes.

桂むきを斜めに切ることで、よりくるくると巻きやすくなる。

Twists can be made harder when Katsura-muki sheet is shredded diagonally.

◆水にさらしてシャキッとさせる
Make Wilted Vegetables Crisp

水にさらすことであくが抜け、その野菜本来の
鮮やかな色が出てシャキッとします。数分さら
してシャキッとしたら取り出し、よく水気をき
ります。また、うどなどのあくの強い野菜は、酢
水にさらしてあく止めをします。

Disagreeable bitterness can be removed from
vegetables by soaking them in water. Soaking may
bring out the natural vivid color. Leave for several
minutes until the pieces become crisp, and drain
well.

水にさらすことで、むきものがハリを取り
戻す。

By soaking in cold water the vegetable will
regain its crispness.

◆塩水に漬けてしんなりさせる
Extract Water with Salty Water

野菜を塩水に漬けると、浸透圧でしんなりとし
ます。柔らかくしたいときや、少ししんなりし
た方がむきやすい場合などに用います。

When you want to create a softer texture or make
something easy to peel, soak the vegetable in salty
water. Salt extracts water by osmotic pressure.

むきにくいときや、割れが心配なときに塩
水に漬けるとむきやすくなる。

When the vegetable is crisp, use this technique
to prevent cracking by making it wilt.

切れ端もムダなく使う
Do Not Throw Away Food Scraps

むきものでは野菜の切れ端が多くでますが、
それらも捨てずにムダなく使いましょう。
それぞれの野菜を料理に使ったり、なんで
も刻んでみそ汁に入れてしまうのもひとつ
の手です。形作っていく前に皮をむくのは、
切れ端をそのまま料理に使えるようにする
ためでもあります。

You might think mukimono creates not only
beauty but also a lot of waste. You can use
vegetable scraps in other recipes such as miso
soups. This is the reason vegetables are peeled
before shaping them into the desired form.

四季の料理を彩る

ADD FLAIR
TO THE SEASON

春夏秋冬、その季節にふさわしいむきものの作り方と
料理がより栄える組み合わせ方を料理例とともに紹介します。
花鳥風月を中心としたむきものを添えて移りゆく季節を感じ、
おいしく食べてもらうことを意識しましょう。

Spring, summer, autumn and winter … each season can be expressed
by mukimono. In this chapter I introduce seasonal mukimono and
suitable combinations to show its best attributes. Always take into
account that the diner can feel the effect of the changing season
through the beauty of nature displayed on the table.

わらびだいこん

Daikon Bracken

わらびだいこんは主に早春の造りに添えるあしらい
で、切れ目を入れて水にさらすと繊維が引っ張られ
て丸くなります。今回は12cm長さにしたものを使い、
6cmのところまで切れ目を入れています。

Warabi, or edible bracken fern shoots, represent early spring, and their fiddlehead
shape will convey the hint of spring. Make scores and soak in cold water until the
fibers are pulled one way. These examples are made of 12cm long stem which has
6cm scores.

だいこんの葉軸を使う。葉を手でむ
しり取る。

Tear off small leafy stems from
daikon.

葉を除いた軸のみを使う。

Use only stem parts.

36

3

軸のくぼんでいる側を下にして置き、小口から細かく切り込みを入れて切り落とさないギリギリのところで止める。

Lay the stem dented side down, make fine deep scores as deep as possible.

4

葉軸の長さの半分ほどまで切り込みを入れる。まな板に接していた部分のみ、つながっている状態。

Make sure the scores are so deep that only the bottom skin is left uncut.

5

両サイドを切り落とし、水に入れたときにより巻くようにする。さらに縦半分に切る。

Cut away both sides lengthwise in order to let it curl deeply. Cut lengthwise in half.

6

水にさらすと、丸まってわらびのようになる。

Soak in cold water until they curl up.

SENMAI OUKA DAIKON
千枚桜花だいこん
<ruby>千<rt>せん</rt>枚<rt>まい</rt>桜<rt>おう</rt>花<rt>か</rt></ruby>
Mille-feuille Cherry Blossoms

幾重にも重なった桜は存在感があり、主役級の
華があります。美しく繊細に仕上げるには、で
きるだけ薄く切ることがポイント。用途に応じ
て必要な厚みに切り離して使います。

Layers of cherry petals have real presence as a
symbol of spring season. The petal layers are
connected at one point, and the required amount can
be cut off according to need. The trick is paper-thin
slicing of the vegetable.

だいこんをむきやすい長さに切り、
皮をむいて五角（P.18）に木取る。

Cut a manageable length of daikon.
Peel and cut out GOKAKU(P.18).

各辺の中央に5㎜ほどの切り込みを
入れる。

Make 5mm deep slit into the center of
each side.

花びらを作る。角から切り込みの深
いところに向かって切る。角はやや
丸めるイメージで包丁を入れる。

Shape petals. Start from the peak and
peel towards the slit. Leave the peaks
slightly round, and not sharp.

花びらの右側だけ1周切った状態。

Only one side of each petal is shaped,
after working around the piece.

手前と向こう側をひっくり返し、同
様に反対側も角から切り込みの深い
ところに向かって切る。

Turn over and repeat on the other side
of the petal, working from the peak
downwards.

桜の花びらが形作れた。花びらの先
端はやや鋭角に残すと桜らしく、丸
くすると梅らしくなる。

Basic shape. Leave the peaks round to
resemble Japanese plum blossom, or
pointed to resemble cherry blossom.

EBI SHINJO USUKUZU-JITATE

えび しんじょう うすくず じたて

海老真丈 薄葛仕立

Thick Soup with Shrimp Dumpling

千枚桜花だいこん　せり　桜花　エビ真丈

Senmai Ouka Daikon　Seri greens
Salted Cherry Blossoms
Shrimp dumplings

エビ真丈の上に千枚桜花だいこんをのせ、上品に仕上げた春の椀。千枚桜花だいこんは花びらを少しずつずらし、重なり合う桜を表現しています。左右に渡したせりと、のせた桜花がアクセントになっています。

An elegant soup with layered cherry petals placed on a shrimp dumpling is perfect for a springtime treat. The petals are placed slightly akew to depict layered cherry blossoms, and natural cherry blossoms on greens add an accent.

7

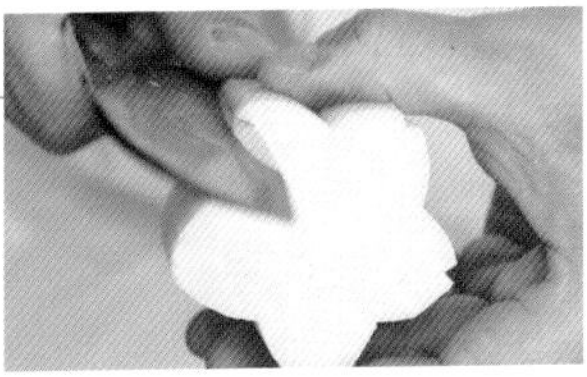

花びらの先端に包丁をＶ字に入れて切り取る。

Make a v-cut on each peak.

8

小口から薄く切り、切り落とさないところで止める。花びらの角の一点だけがつながったままにする。

Slice thinly, but do not cut through completely, so that the petals remain joined at the bottom point.

9

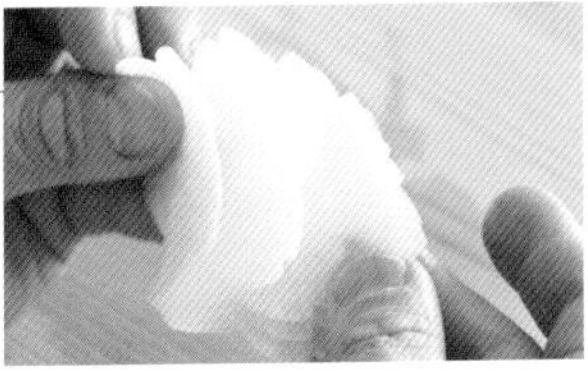

下がわずかにつながったまま、桜の花びらが何枚も重なった状態。

Petals are separate and connect only at the bottom point.

10

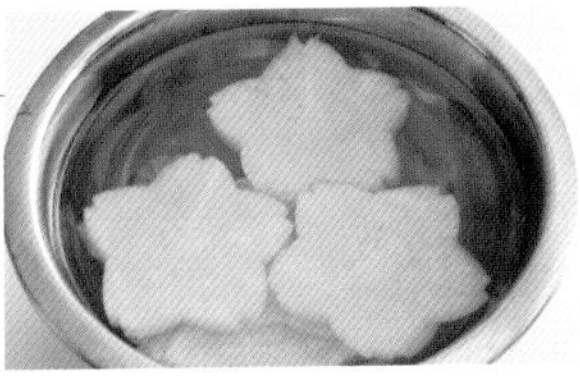

水にさらしてシャキッとさせる。

Soak in cold water until crisp.

だいこんけん

Shredded Daikon

だいこんの繊維に対して直角に切ったけん（細く切る）は「横けん」、繊維に添って切ったけんは「縦けん」と呼びます。この横けんは、下に敷いたりふわっとしたボリュームを出すときに用います。

When daikon is shredded against its grain, it is called "YOKO KEN," or horizontal shreds. When shredded along its grain, then it is "TATE KEN," or vertical shreds. Yoko ken which is introduced here is useful for raising main food or when fluffy shreds are required.

1

薄く桂むき（P.22）しただいこんを使う。

Make Katsura-muki(p.22) daikon sheet.

2

長さを半分に切って重ねる。

Cut the length in half and layer.

3

使いたい長さに合わせて切る。これは約5cm。

Cut to required length. For the salad, cut into 5cm lengths.

4

同じ大きさに切りそろえる。

Cut into the same lengths.

5

適当な枚数を重ね、繊維を横にしてまな板に置く。

Layer appropriate amount sheets so that the grain lies sideways.

6

サラダなので少し太めの千切りにして水にさらし、シャキッとさせて水気をきる。

For salads, cut into slightly thicker shreds than you would for sashimi garnish.Soak in cold water until crisp.

春物サラダ仕立
Spring Salad

だいこんけん　にんじんけん　きゅうりけん　ホタルイカ
シラウオワカメ　木の芽　こごみ　アスパラ　たけのこ　梅肉

Daikon Ken　Ninjin Ken　Kyuri Ken　Asparagas
Bamboo shoot　Firefly squid　Japanese icefish　Wakame seaweed
Kinome sprigs　Kogomi fern　Pickled plum paste

春の野菜と魚介を花畑のようなサラダにしました。柔らかな
色味の3種のけんが、色とりどりの湯通しした食材と調和し
て春らしい空気を作り出しています。黄色の酢みそと赤の梅
肉がアクセントに。

Spring vegetables and seafood assorted into a refreshing salad
resembling a flowering meadow. Pale shades of Ken shreds
create a springtime air in harmony with colorful morsels that are
blanched.

にんじんけん
Shredded Carrots

にんじんけんは繊維に添って切り、「縦けん」にしました。けんをサラダに用いるときには少し太めに、造りには極細い千切りにするなど、用途に応じて変えましょう。

Carrot is shredded along the grain to make Tate ken. Make a little thicker shreds for salads, or fine shreds to accompany Sashimi.

1

にんじんを使いたいけんの長さに切り、皮をむく。

Cut into a manageable length, and peel off the skin.

2

太さを均等にする。

Peel around, keeping the width of the cylinder even.

3

薄く桂むき（P.22）する。

Continue to work Katsura-muki(p.22) thinly until the desired amount is reached.

4

同じ大きさに切りそろえて重ねる。

Cut into evenly sized sheets and layer them.

5

繊維に添って千切りにして水にさらし、シャキッとさせて水気をきる。

Shred along the grain. Soak in cold water until the shreds become crisp.

42

KYURI KEN

きゅうりけん

Shredded Cucumber

桂むきにして中心の種を除き、繊維に添って切ります。皮はやや硬いので、軽くむいて口当たりをよくしましょう。だいこん、にんじんのけんと合わせて用いれば、料理が華やかになります。

Peel Katsura-muki from cucumber and remove the seeds. Peel the skin roughly for a tender texture. Combine with daikon or carrot shreds when a colorful display is needed.

1

きゅうりを使いたいけんの長さに切る。

Cut cucumber into needed size.

2

軽く皮をむく。

Peel thinly, partially leaving the green skin.

3

皮をむき、太さを整えた状態。

Check that it is evenly thick around for easy peeling.

4

薄い桂むき（P.22）にする。

Work Katsura-muki(P.22) and make a thin sheet.

5

種のある中心部分は除く。

Remove the seeded core.

6

適当な長さに切って重ね、一度にたくさん切れるようにする。

Cut into appropriate lengths, and layer the sheets.

7

繊維に添って千切りにして水にさらし、シャキッとさせて水気をきる。

Shred along the grain. Soak in cold water until the shreds become crisp.

43

花びらゆり根
Lily Bulb Cherry Petals

ゆり根の鱗片の丸みと形を生かし、桜の花びらにむきます。食用色素入りの水でゆでると、切り口にだけ色が入りより雰囲気が出ます。他の部分に色がつかないのは、ゆり根が皮膜に覆われているからです。

To make the best of Yurine, or edible lily bulb, make each scale into a petal shape. Only the edges will take on a delicate pink color when cooked in water with a pinch food color. The trick is the filmy skin that covers the scales.

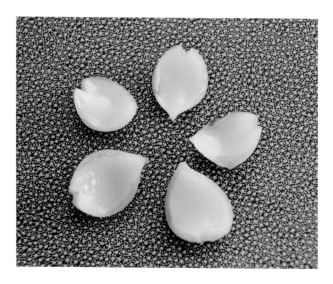

1

ゆり根を1枚ずつはがす。外側の大きな鱗片よりも少し内側のやや小ぶりな鱗片を使うとよい。

Separate each scale of the edible lily bulb. Avoid outer scales and use small inner ones.

2

鱗片の形を生かし、花びらの形をかたどる。

Check the shape of scale to make the most of its contour.

3

鱗片の先端に包丁を入れ、輪郭を整える。

Beginning at the tip, cut a side.

4

包丁は一息に動かしてシャープで勢いのあるラインを作る。

Move the knife in one smooth motion and create a sharp streamline.

5

反対サイドも同様に整える。

Repeat on the other side.

6

花びらの輪郭を整えた状態。

The contour of the petal.

7

花びらの先端になる部分に包丁を入れ、Ⅴ字に切り取る。

Insert the knife into the tip of petal, and cut away a tiny v-shape.

8

花びらの形が完成。

Completed petal shape.

9

鍋に水と少量の食用色素を入れ、8のゆり根をゆでると皮膜を切り取った部分だけがピンクに染まる。

In a pan put water and little food color. Boil the shaped petals until the cut edges are dyed pink.

花びらしょうが
Ginger Flower Petals

桜の花びらをしょうがで表現しました。さっと湯通しして甘酢に漬ければ、口直しのガリになります。甘酢に漬けるとほんのりピンク色に染まり、風情ある添え物に。

Cherry blossom petals made from fresh ginger root. Blanch sliced ginger petals briefly in boiling water and dip in sweet vinegar to naturally turn the petals to pale pink. These ginger petals make an attractive and refreshing relish.

1 しょうがの細い部分を切り落とす。

Cut away narrow section of fresh ginger root.

2 しょうがは使いたい大きさに合った部分を用いる。

Cut roughly into size needed for petals.

3

皮をむく。

Remove the skin.

4

花びらの形をイメージしながら、粗く削る。

To create the image of layered petals, roughly trim away around the sides.

5

大まかな花びらの形をかたどった状態。

Roughly shaped block of ginger.

6

両サイドの花びらの輪郭を整える。

Adjust the contour of petals by peeling one side each.

7

包丁を一息に動かし、シャープな曲線を描いて花びらの形をかたどる。

Do not hesitate when slicing. Slice in one motion to create a sharp streamline.

8

花びらの先端になる部分に包丁を入れ、V字に切り取る。

Trim away v-shape from each tip.

9

花びらの形が決まった状態。

Petal block is completed.

10

包丁使いにカーブをつけ、やや厚め（ここでは2㎜ほど）にむいて花びらを作る。

Peel off a slightly thick petal (2mm here).

花見手まり寿し

Mini Sushi Balls for Cherry Blossom Viewing

花びらゆり根　花びらしょうが　タイ昆布〆
サヨリ　アナゴ　エビ　トリ貝　木の芽

Hanabira Yurine　Hanabira Shoga　Marinated sea bream
Sayori fish　Cooked sea eel　Prawn　Shellfish　Kinome sprigs

ひと口サイズのかわいらしい寿司に、花びらをかたどったゆり根としょうがを添え、春の宴を表現しました。ピンク色に染まったゆり根としょうがが、いままさに花見をしているかのように気分を盛り上げてくれます。

Fallen cherry petals in pale pink adorn this party dish with bite-size sushi balls. The petals are made of fresh ginger and edible lily bulbs.

JUNSAI IMO-OTOSHI

じゅん菜芋落とし

Sunken Taro in Junsai Greens

らせんきゅうり　アワビ　ホタテ　じゅん菜　山いも
ラディッシュ　しょうが酢

Rasen Kyuri　Radish　Junsai sprouts　Scallops　Abalone
Yam　Ginger vinegar

6月から8月に旬を迎え、夏の訪れを感じさせるじゅん菜を
らせんきゅうりで変化をつけて飾りました。ツルツルとした
じゅん菜と異なる食感の食材の組み合わせが楽しい、さっぱ
りといただける夏の先附です。

A summery appetizer featuring Junsai, or water shield, decorated
with playful Rasen Kyuri. The combination of Slipppery and
crisp textures adds fun.

49

RASEN KYURI

らせんきゅうり

Cucumber Spirals

きゅうりの中心を筒抜きで抜き、切り込みを入れてらせん状に。飾るだけで料理に変化がつく、動きのある形のむきものです。

Remove the center of cucumber using Tsutsu-nuki and make cuts. This mukimono adds movement to ordinary dishes.

1

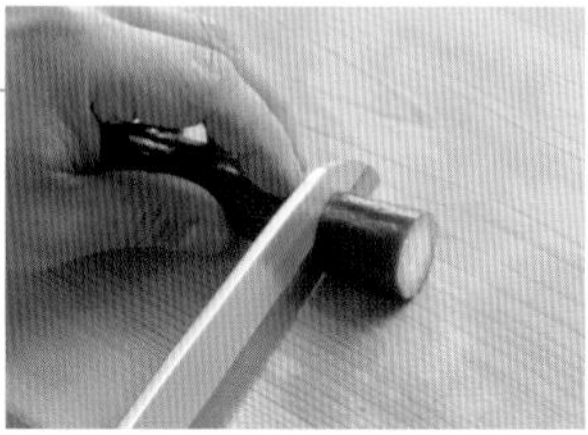

きゅうりを必要な長さに切る。中を筒抜きで抜ける長さにしておく。

Cut a length of Japanese cucumber, checking that it is not longer than the Tsutsu-nuki. Choose a right size Tsutsu-nuki.

2

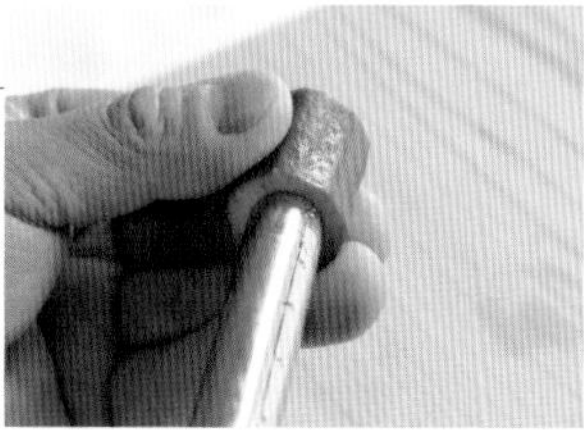

筒抜きを片側から差し込み、半分を越えたら反対側から差し込んで中を抜く。両側から筒抜きを差すときれいに抜ける。

Insert Tsutsu-nuki into one end. When inserted to little over the middle, remove and insert from the other end.

3

きゅうりにサイズを合わせた筒抜きで、中の種を抜き取った状態。

This way you can make a fine tube.

4

きゅうりを横にして置き、小口から3mm幅に切れ目を入れる。

Lay cucumber down, and make 3mm wide cuts, but do not cut through.

5

まな板に接地している部分は切り離さず、つなげておく。

Leave the very bottom touching the cutting board uncut. Repeat until the end.

6

手前の切れ目に刃先を入れ、左隣りの奥側の切れ目とつなげるように斜めに切る。

Insert knife tip into the first slit made, and slice at a slant away from you, to connect to the next slit on the far side.

7

ひとつ切り離した状態。

One layer has been separated.

8

同様にすべての切れ目を切り離す。

Repeat until all the slits are connected.

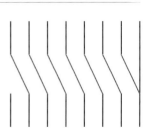

手前の切れ目から刃先を入れ、左隣りの奥側の切れ目に刃先を入れて斜めに切り落とす。

Insert knife into the near side of slit, working away from you, then cut diagonally to separate a circle.

CHO NINJIN

蝶にんじん
Carrot Butterflies

ひらひらと舞う蝶をにんじんで立体的に表現しています。間に切り込みを入れて薄く切り、羽の間に触角を入れ込んで立体的に。料理に添えれば、春を感じさせる華やかな雰囲気になります。

Fluttering butterflies are re-created in 3D. Deep slits between wing-shaped thin slices of carrot will form the butterfly feelers. Add to your dish to herald spring.

1

にんじんをむきやすい長さに切り、皮をむいて4等分し、いちょう(P.14)に木取る。

Cut carrot into a manageable length. Peel and split into Icho(P.14), or quarters.

2

蝶の触角部分を作る。弧を左にして置き、薄く切り込みを入れて切り落とさないところで止める。

Make feelers. Lay the Icho block round side on your left, and slice very thinly until almost cut through, but not completely.

3

切り落とさず、2㎜ほどつながったままになるよう、包丁を入れる。

Side view of the block, leaving 2mm uncut.

4

手前と向こう側をひっくり返し、2と同様に反対側からも切り込みを入れて切り落とさないところで止める。

Turn over so that the front end is away from you. Repeat step 2, leaving 2mm uncut.

5

2つの切れ目が入り、互い違いに切れている(図)。

Two deep slits are made alternately. (See bottom right figure.)

6

蝶の羽を作る。にんじんを横に置き、薄く切り込みを入れて切り落とさないところで止める。

Make wings from the same block. Slice Icho face very thinly until almost cut, but not completely.

7

2度目は同じ薄さで包丁を入れ、切り離す。

Slice the same width, and cut through to make a pair of wings. Repeat steps 6 and 7.

8

蝶を平面でむいた状態。

Butterfly wings made this way will stay closely folded.

9

羽の切り込みを指でやさしく開く。

Gently open the wings with your fingers.

10

触角の下の部分を羽の間に押し込む。

Push the bottom of the feelers between the wings.

11

羽の先を指で押し広げ、触角の先を指で押さえて形を整える。

Push open the wings, and adjust the position of the feelers.

12

羽が丸みを帯び、触角もピンと広がって立体的な蝶になった。

A 3D butterfly with rounded wings and straight feelers is formed.

13

水にさらすと、もう少し羽にそりが出て広がりシャキッとする。

For more 3D and stiffer effect, soak in cold water and drain.

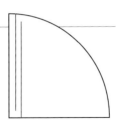

触角部分は互い違いに切り込みを入れる。切り落とさないように2mmほどつなげておく。

Create feelers by making deep slits alternately, leaving 2mm uncut each.

RASEN RADISH

らせん ラディッシュ
Radish Spirals

ラディッシュのヒゲ根と葉を切り落とす。

Trim away stems and roots of radish.

ラディッシュにサイズを合わせた筒抜きで、中を抜く。

Using an appropriate size Tsutsu-nuki, remove the center.

ラディッシュを横にして置き、端から3㎜幅に切れ目を入れ、まな板に接地している部分は切り離さず、つなげておく。

Lay the radish on a cutting board sideways, and cut 3mm slices almost through but not completely. Repeat to the end.

手前の切れ目に刃先を入れ、左隣りの奥側の切れ目とつなげるように斜めに切る。水にさらしてシャキッとさせる。

Insert knife tip into the first slit made, and slice at a slant away from you, to connect to the next slit on the far side. Soak in cold water to let it crisp.

HANA RADISH

花ラディッシュ
Radish Floret

 1

ラディッシュの真ん中あたりの皮を
小さく丸く切り取る。均等に1周で
5カ所取る。

Slice away a tiny circle from the fattest
middle part, evenly 5 spots around.

 2

丸く切り取った部分に下から包丁を
入れる。

Insert knife just underneath the tiny
white circle, and make a slit.

 3

赤い皮がふちとして残る程度の大き
さで2回包丁を入れる。

Make another slit under the slit just
made, leaving only a thin semi-circle
of red remaining.

4

ラディッシュの底に包丁をV字に入
れて切り取り、3本筋を入れる。水
にさらすと切れ目が開き、花のよう
になる。

Into the bottom of the radish, cut a
v-shaped score. Repeat twice to make
an asterisk.
Soak in cold water until the floret
"blooms," and drain.

水玉ラディッシュ

Radish Swirl

赤い皮のふちが残るように、横にぐるぐるとむいて形を戻したむきものです。皮の赤と丸いフォルムがかわいらしい印象を与えます。葉つきのまま飾れば、高さが出て料理の見栄えがよくなります。

The color contrast is emphasized by peeling the sides of radish. The round shape and the thin red accent together make a cute impression. Place on a plate with leafy stems to create a sense of height.

1

ラディッシュは底を薄く切り落とし、座りをよくする。

Slice off bottom thinly to create a level base.

2

真ん中から薄く細くむく。

Beginning at the middle fat part, peel thinly around.

56

3

２周目は、ふちに赤い皮のラインが
残るようにやや幅を広くしてむく。

On the second round, peel wider so
that red lines show.

4

上下ギリギリまでむく。

Peel until you have to stop, both at top
and bottom.

5

ラディッシュを薄く横にむいた状態。

A long thin strip of peel.

6

むいたものをくるくると元に戻す。

Wrap the strip around the center, back
in the original position.

7

水にさらしてシャキッとさせる。

Soak in cold water until crisp; drain.

DENDEN KYURI

でんでんきゅうり
Cucumber Snails

きゅうりを桂むきにした簡単なむきものですが、料理
や他のむきものと組み合わせることで世界観が生ま
れます。やや厚めに切り分けると、よりかたつむりら
しさが表現できます。

Although this is a simple mukimono, you can make a charming display in
combination with different shapes of food. Slice slightly thicker for more realism.

1

きゅうりはへたを切り落とし、必要
な長さに切る。

Trim away cucumber stem, and cut a
manageable length.

2

薄く皮をむく。

Peel thinly.

3

厚めの桂むき (P.22) にする。

Make a thick Katsura-muki (P.22).

4

種ギリギリのところで包丁を止め、
つなげたままにする。

Continue until you reach seed section,
but do not cut off.

AJISAI MORI

あじさい盛り
SASHIMI HYDRANGEAS

でんでんきゅうり　あじさい酢立　イカ　マグロ
きゅうり　山いも　たで（赤・緑）　花穂じそ

Denden Kyuri　Citrus cups　Squid sashimi
Tuna sashimi　Cucumber　Yam　Knotweed
Flowering shiso sprigs

花盛りのあじさいとそこに現
れたかたつむりで、梅雨時期
の情景を表現しました。色鮮
やかな満開のあじさいは、あ
られ切りにしたイカ、マグロ、
きゅうり、山いもを和えたも
のです。

Japanese rainy season offers
beautiful hydrangea hues and
wet green leaves on which
you often find cute snails.
The vibrant colors of the
hydrangeas come from tuna,
squid, cucumber and yam, cut
into tiny cubes.

5

切ったものをくるくると元に戻し、
太めの輪切りにする。

Roll the strip around the center, back to
the beginning, and cut.

6

厚めの輪切りにした状態。これは7
mm厚さほど。

Cut into thick rounds, 7mm wide here.

7

水にさらしてシャキッとさせる。

Soak in cold water until crisp; drain.

よりにんじん
Carrot Twists

桂むきしたにんじんを斜めに細く切り、箸などに巻きつけて形作ってから氷水にさらして形を固定させます。造りや酢の物のあしらいに彩りを添えるむきものです。

Peel carrot into Katsura-muki, slice thinly, and fix the twist using chopstick and ice water.
Decorate sashimi or salad dishes with these to add color and twist.

1

にんじんの細い部分を使う。カーブが強いので、よりにしたときに巻きやすい。

Use narrower part of carrot since its natural curve helps the twist fix.

2

薄く皮をむく。

Peel the skin thinly.

3

桂むき（P.22）をする。けんにするときよりも厚めに、厚さを均等にむく。

Peel Katsura-muki(P.22) thicker than you would for Ken.

4

まな板に桂むきを広げ、斜めに細く切る（図）。

Spread the sheet out and cut thinly at a slant (see bottom right figure).

5

よりは細く長い方が存在感が出る。

The thinner and longer the twists, the more expressive they look.

6

箸に巻きつけ、指先に力を入れて形作る。

Wrap the strip around a chopstick, and press hard.

7

箸に巻きつけて形作った状態。

Twist is being formed.

8

氷水に入れて形を固定させる。冷たい水の方が形が決まりやすい。

Soak in cold water to fix the shape. (The colder, the better.)

桂むきを斜めになるべく長く取れるように切る。野菜の繊維の方向を利用してよりにする。

Cut at a slant, as long as you can. Make twists using the natural fiber direction of the vegetable.

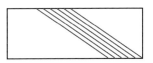

YORI KYURI

よりきゅうり
Cucumber Twists

にんじんと同じ要領でよりを作ります。きゅうりは皮を薄くむくことで濃い色が残り、よりに表情がつきます。にんじんやだいこんなど、色の違う野菜と合わせて用いると華やかな印象に。

Make Katsura-muki sheet of Japanese cucumber. Shred and wrap around a stick, and then soak in cold water stabilize the shape.

1

きゅうりはへたを落とし、必要な長さに切る。

Trim away edge of Japanese cucumber and cut into a length needed.

2

包丁を上下に動かしながら皮を薄くむく。

Peel the skin thinly, moving the knife upwards and downwards.

3

やや皮が残っている方が色に濃淡がつき、表情がつく。

The green skin partially remains,which will give contrast and expression.

4

厚めに桂むき (P.22) をする。厚さを
均等にむく。

Make a thick Katsura-muki(P.22). Keep
an even thickness.

5

種の外側まで桂むきにする。

Continue until the knife reaches the
seeded center.

6

まな板に桂むきを広げ、斜めに細く
切る。

Lay the sheet down and cut thinly at
a slant.

7

刃先を使い、包丁を引きながら切る。

Using the tip of the knife, cut with
drawing motion.

8

箸に巻きつけ、指先に力を入れる。

Wrap around a chopstick, and press
hard.

9

指先で全体をよって形作る。

Using your fingertips, twist the whole
strip.

10

氷水に入れて形を固定させる。冷た
い水の方が形が決まりやすい。

Soak in cold water to fix the shape.
(The colder the water, the stiffer the shapes.)

よりだいこん
Daikon Twists

真っすぐなだいこんは、ある程度の長さを一度に桂むきしやすく、桂むきを重ねて斜めに切ると、一度に大量のよりを作ることができます。生で食べられる野菜のよりやけんは、造りなどに添えて口直しに。

Daikon's straight characteristic makes knife work easy and you can peel several wide Katsura-muki at one time by layering the sheets and cutting at a slant. Any vegetable eaten raw can be made into twists or shreds, which will make a refreshing garnish for sashimi.

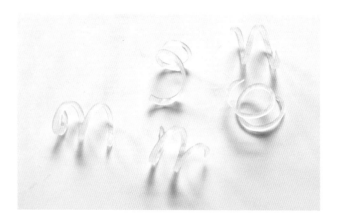

1

だいこんはむきやすい長さに切り、皮をむいて厚めの桂むき（P.22）にする。

Cut a manageable length of daikon. Remove the skin, and then peel into a slightly thick Katsura-muki(P.22).

2

桂むきを必要な長さと幅に切り、重ねる。

Stack Katsura-muki sheets and cut into desired lengths and widths.

3

斜めに細く切る。重ねて切ることで、一度にたくさん作ることができる。

Slice thinly at a slant. Layer sheets for quicker work.

HAMO OTOSHI

はもおとし
鱧落し

Kyoto Eel Salad

よりにんじん　よりきゅうり　よりだいこん
鱧　大葉　花穂じそ　梅肉
Yori Ninjin　Yori Kyuri　Yori Daikon,
Hamo (pike conger)　Shiso leaves
Flowering shiso sprigs
Pickled plum paste

京都の夏に欠かせない鱧は、
皮を切らずに細かく包丁を入
れて小骨を切断する骨切りを
し、湯引きして梅肉で。さっ
ぱりとした夏にぴったりの料
理です。色味の少ない鱧に、3
色のよりを添えて華やかに仕
上げました。

Hamo, summer delicacy of
Kyoto, boiled and served with
refreshing pickled plum sauce.
Vegetable twists in three colors
enhance this colorless delicacy.

よりは細く長い方が存在感が出る。

The longer the twists, the more
expressive they look.

指先で全体をよって形作る。

Using your fingertips, twist the whole
strip.

箸に巻きつけ、指先に力を入れて形
作る。

Wrap the strip around a chopstick, and
press hard.

氷水に入れて形を固定させる。冷た
い水の方が形が決まりやすい。

Soak in cold water to fix the shape.
(The colder, the better.)

65

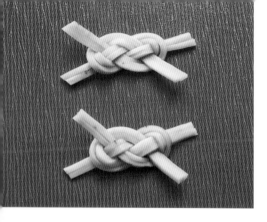

MUSUBI GOBO

結びごぼう
Gobo Knots

ゆでたごぼうを組んで結ぶ結びごぼうは、慶事に用いられるおめでたいむきものです。甘酢に漬けて、酢ごぼうにします。

Cooked gobo, or burdock, is made into a double knot, which is a symbol of union, thus these often decorate dishes at wedding and anniversaries.

1

ごぼうは20cmほどに切る。ある程度長さがないと結びにくい。

Cut gobo into 20cm lengths. Take enough length for tying later.

2

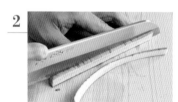

3mmほどの厚さで縦に切る。

Cut lengthwise into 3mm thicknesses.

3

寝かせてまな板に置き、刃先で半分に切る。

Lay on a cutting board. Using the tip of knife, cut into halves in a smooth, drawing motion.

4

上を切り落とさず、中央に切れ目を入れる。

Cut again in half, this time leaving the beginning uncut.

5

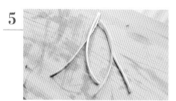

切れ目を入れた状態。太さはそろえる。

Two strips with deep slits. Check that they have the same width.

6

下ゆでし、小さな輪を作って両手に
持つ。

Boil briefly and make a loop. Hold one
in each hand.

7

右の輪を左上の端にかける。

Bring the loop in your right hand over
one end of your left-hand loop.

8

右上の端を抜き、左の輪の下から上
へ通し、ごぼうを上下と縫うように
通して組む。

Pull out right-hand end towards you,
and pass through the loop in your left
hand.

9

粗く組んだ状態。

Loosely braided strips.

10

左右をバランスよく引いて徐々にき
つく結ぶ。

Pull each evenly, little by little,
outwards.

11

バランスよく結んだ状態。

The result should be in balance.

12

端を切ってそろえる。

Trim away ends.

赤の輪を青の左上の端にかけ、赤の右上
の端（★）を一度開く。

Hook red loop on upper left end of blue
loop, and bring the end of red (★) to upper
right.

赤の右上の端（★）を青の輪の下部分に下
から通し、赤の右下の端の上を通り、青
の輪の上部分の下へ通す。

Pass the end of red (★) under the blue loop
and over the red, and then under the upper
section of the blue loop. Pull both ends.

管 ごぼう
<small>かん</small>

Gobo Tubes

ごぼうの栄養価や旨みは、そのほとんどが皮や皮の近くに多く含まれます。柔らかく
下ゆですると、竹串で簡単に中を抜くことができ、ごぼうのおいしいところを残した
まま手軽にできるむきものです。

Gobo has a distinctively pleasant crunchiness and flavor that are contained within and near
the skin. The center can be removed easily using a stick after being parboiled. This is an
easy mukimono to use to offer the tasty part of this root vegetable.

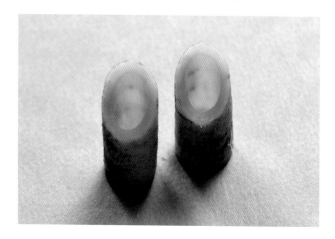

1

ごぼうはぬかを入れて柔らかく下ゆでし、ごぼうの断面に見える輪に沿って竹串を刺す。

Parboil gobo until tender. Using a bamboo skewer, pierce along the inner circle of the cut edge.

2

ごぼうの輪に沿って竹串を動かす。

Move the skewer around in a circular motion to separate the center from the outer circle.

3

竹串を両側から刺して輪に沿って動かすと、簡単に中が抜ける。

Repeat on the other cut edge, and the center will come away.

4

きれいにごぼうの中だけが抜けた状態。

The tube and the center just removed.

5

中を抜いたごぼうを斜め半分に切る。

Halve the gobo tube at a slant.

6

用途や器に合わせて長さを変えるとよい。

Alter the height according to purpose or serving container.

HORAKU KO-KABU

宝楽小かぶ
ほうらくこ

Stuffed Turnip

松葉ゆず　六方小かぶ　茶碗蒸し　エビ　ぎんなん　しめじ

Matsuba Yuzu　Roppo Kokabu　Savory egg custard
Prawn　Gingko nuts　Shimeji mushrooms

10月から12月に秋かぶは旬を迎え、たっぷりと甘みを蓄えます。
小かぶを器に仕立て、茶碗蒸しを入れて器ごと食べられる一品に。
松葉ゆずで香りを添え、かぶのふたとともに盛りつけました。

October to December is the best season for autumn kabu, or white
turnips, when they natural sweetness increases. A tiny Japanese turnip
made into a container to hold delicate savory custard can be eaten
whole. Display with the "lid" and aromatic Matsuba Yuzu.

ROPPO KO-KABU
六方小かぶ
ろっぽうこ
Hexagonal White Turnip Cups

小かぶを六方にむいて中をくり抜き、器に仕立てました。入れる料理の量に合わせてくり抜く深さや大きさを変えましょう。ふたの作り方が異なる2パターンを紹介します。

Small kabu, or Japanese turnip, made into a charming container. Adjust the size of the space depending on the amount of filling. Here are two patterns and different procedures for lid making.

◆後でふたを作る To Make the Lid Later

1

茎を3㎝ほど残し、かぶの葉を切る。

Cut away the leaves, at 3cm from the turnip.

2

かぶの下部を厚めに切り落とす。

Slice off the bottom of turnip.

3

下から六方（P.20）にむく。かぶは皮の内側に筋があるので、口当たりをよくするため、皮を厚くむく。

Peel to form Roppo(P.20) on. Make a thick slice to remove the fibrous section under the skin.

4

茎の手前で包丁を止め、包丁を一度外して茎に沿って切れ目を入れ、皮を切り落とす。

Stop peeling before reaching the stem. Insert knife into the edges of stem, and peel towards the kabu.

5

同様に皮をむいていく。

Repeat on the other 5 sides.

6

六方にむいた状態。

Roppo is formed.

7

茎を切り落とし、ふたを作る。

Cut the upper part to make the lid.

8

いも抜きをかぶにかぶせるようにして当て、手首を回転させて中身を抜く。

Using a baller, scoop out the inside in a rotating motion.

9

かぶの大きさに合わせていも抜きのサイズを選び、丸く抜く。

Choose an appropriate size baller for the size of turnip.

◆ 先にふたを作る To Make the Lid First

1

茎を切り落とし、ふたにする。

Cut off the upper part to make the lid.

2

かぶの下部を厚めに切り落とし、上から六方にむく。

Cut away the bottom of turnip, and make a thick slice from the top, downwards.

3

1のふたも茎の周りを六方にむく。

Peel the lid into Roppo in the same manner.

4

いも抜きで中身をくり抜く。

Scoop out the inside using a baller.

KIKYO KYURI

桔梗 きゅうり
き きょう
Cucumber Bellflowers

一息にむき、勢いのあるラインで桔梗の花を表現しましょう。1本のきゅうりから連続していくつも作ることができます。薬味を入れて添えると、見栄えがするあしらいとなります。

Try to peel the cucumber in a single motion to create neat and sharp lines of petals. You can make many out of a cucumber continuously. This will make a showy cup for any condiment you add to your dish.

1

きゅうりのへたを切り落とす。

Trim away the stem of the cucumber.

2

先端の周りの苦みがある部分をむく。

Peel off the skin under the stem, as it may taste bitter.

74

3

ペティナイフの刃先を使って細く5本の皮をむく。

Using the tip of petty knife, peel off 5 narrow strips of skin, evenly spaced.

4

3の細い線ごと上から切れ目を入れ、切り離さずに最後は手首を返して刃先を内側に入れる。

Insert knife at a slant, making a deep slit underneath the peeled section just made. Do not cut through, and rotate your wrist inwards to end at the bottom.

5

5カ所すべてを同様にむく。

Repeat on all 5 sections.

6

ふきんで押さえ、ひねって外す。

Holding the cucumber with a towel, twist off the uncut part of cucumber.

7

ねじって外した状態。

The first flower is separated.

8

まな板に寝せて置き、花びら一枚一枚の輪郭をペティナイフの刃先で鋭く整える。

Lay the flower on a cutting board, and trim tips of petals to make them sharp and pointed.

9

花びらを整えた状態。

Check that the petals are sharply trimmed.

10

花びらを指でつまみ、外向きに広がるようにくせをつける。

Curl each petal outwards by pulling with your fingers.

11

ひとつ外したきゅうりは、4と同様に5カ所包丁を入れる。

Continue to make the second flower, starting with the first cut.

12

ふきんで押さえ、2個目をひねってはずす。

Using a towel, twist off the second flower.

13

花びら一枚一枚の輪郭を鋭く整える。

Trim to shape the petals sharp and pointed.

14

花びらを指でつまみ、外向きに広がるようにくせをつける。

Curl the petals outwards.

15

きゅうりは、皮のない黄緑色の部分が長くなったらそこを切り落とし、また同じ手順で桔梗きゅうりを作る。

Continue until peeled section is too long to manage. Cut off the section and repeat the procedure.

16

水にさらすと花びらが開き、シャキッとする。

Soak in cold water to make them "bloom" and crisp.

KIKKA YUZU

菊花ゆず
<small>（きっ　か）</small>

Yuzu Chrythanthemums

ゆずの香りを存分に生かして料理を引き立てる釜（器）
です。上から1/3あたりを切り、包み込むような形を
作りましょう。切り離した上部は、ふたとしても使
うことができます。

This "kama," or food container, makes the most of the yuzu. Make the cup to
resemble holding something with both of your hands. Top section is cut off, and
can be made into the lid.

1

ゆずの底を薄く切り、座りをよくする。

Cut away a thin slice from the bottom
of yuzu.

2

ペティナイフでゆずの上から1/3の
ところを切る。

Measure one-third from the top to
begin marking the skin with a petty
knife.

78

3

刃先を使い、細く細かい菊の花びら
をイメージする。

Keeping in mind the image of narrow
chrysanthemum petals, insert the tip of
the petty knife and "draw."

4

細かくジグザグにペティナイフを入
れて切る。

Make zigzag scores deeply, reaching
the center.

5

1周切れたらふたを外す。

When you have worked all around,
remove top.

6

スプーンを入れ、周りから中心に果
肉を集めてかき出す。

Using a spoon, scoop out the inside,
scraping the inner skin.

7

白わたまできれいにかき出し、釜の
内部を整える。

Remove white membrane as well until
the inside is clean and smooth.

KIKKA YUZUGAMA-MORI SANSHU

菊花ゆず釜盛り三種

In Chrysanthemum Yuzu Cups

菊花ゆず　いくらのみぞれ和え　イカとわけぎのぬた　エビとしめじの菊花和え
Kikka Yuzu　Ikura with grated radish　Squid and green onion salad　Shrimp and mushroom salad

ペティナイフを使って皮を細かい花びらのようにむいて菊の花に見立て
ました。ゆずの果肉をくり抜き、釜に仕立てています。釜に和え物を詰
め、ゆずのさわやかな香りとともに楽しんでいただける料理です。

Yuzu citron cups with pointed "petals" showcase delicacies not only visually
but also with the tangy fragrance.

80

胡麻豆腐
Sesame Tofu

銀杏かぼちゃ　紅葉にんじん　エビ　旨だし
わさび　胡麻　みそ

Icho Kabocha　Momiji Ninjin　Prawn
Thick dashi sauce　Wasabi　Sesame seeds　Miso

一年を通して手に入るごまですが、旬は収穫を迎える秋。旬の胡麻で作ったなめらかで濃厚なごま豆腐に、銀杏かぼちゃと紅葉にんじんを添えて風情ある一皿に仕上げました。

Sesame seeds are now available all through the year, but autumn is the harvest season when they give the richest aroma. Smooth sesame seed jelly served here is adorned with changing leaves that are actually squash carrot and squash slices.

ICHO KABOCHA
銀杏かぼちゃ
Squash Gingko Leaves

かぼちゃで色づいた銀杏を表現しました。わずかに残った皮の緑が、リアルな雰囲気を作り出しています。秋を象徴するむきもののひとつです。

Yellow colored gingko leaves made from squash are one of the symbols of autumn. Hints of green skin creates a realistic presentation.

1

半分にしたかぼちゃの端を必要な大きさに切る。

Halve a squash and cut into the size as needed.

2

上下を落とし、銀杏の形に整える。

Trim away narrow edges to make a fan shape.

3

皮の中央に3㎜ほどの切れ目を入れる。

Make a 3mm-deep incision into the center of the skin.

4

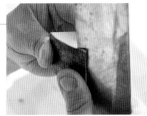

外側から中央の切れ目に向かって皮を薄くむきながら丸みをつける。

Peel a very thin layer of the skin from the edge towards the incision to create a rounded shape.

5

中央は切れ目の深いところに向けて包丁を軽く入れ、皮を切り離す。

Cut a notch using the incision, and remove skin.

6

反対側も同様に丸みをつけながら皮をむく。

Repeat on the other side.

7

丸みをつけて皮をむいた状態。中央に向かってＶ字に切り込みが入っている。

Peeled block with rounded edges and v-incision in the center.

8

角すべてを軽く面取りする。

Round off any corners.

9

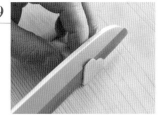

端から薄く切る。

Slice thinly.

10

水にさらしてシャキッとさせる。

Soak in cold water until crisp.

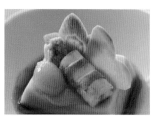

MOMIJI NINJIN
紅葉にんじん
もみじ
Autumn Leaf Carrots

秋と言えば色が日に日に変化していく紅葉が美しいシーズン。鮮やかなにんじんの色味を生かし、紅葉をかたどりました。七角形から作る、葉の長さとバランスがポイントです。

Autumn is a beautiful season when the tree leaves change color day by day. The vividly colored carrots are made into small sized Japanese maple leaves here. The trick is the balance of different sizes of each "tooth."

1

にんじんは必要な長さに切って皮をむき、2辺がやや長めの七角形に木取る（図A）。

Cut a length of carrot you need, peel the skin, and make a heptagon-shaped block (fig.A overleaf).

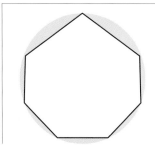

図A
丸の中に七角形を木取る。隣り合った2辺をやや長めにしておく。

Fig. A
Cut out heptagon from the circle. Make 2 sides slightly longer than the others.

2

七角形に木取った状態。

Heptagonal column is cut out.

3

隣り合う同じ長さの5辺の中央に3㎜ほどの切れ目を入れる。

Into the center of 5 shorter sides, make 3mm-deep incisions.

4

残る2辺の間の角が葉の一番先になる。上から3：1になるところに3㎜ほどの切り込みを入れる（図B）。

On the remaining 2 longer sides, make 3mm-deep incisions three quarters down from the top corner. This will form the largest "tooth" of the leaf(Fig. B).

図B
上の2辺は3：1のところに切り込みを入れ、他5辺は中央に切り込みを入れ、つなぐように紅葉形にむく。

Fig. B
Make an incision three quarters down from the top on both of the top sides. On the other 5 sides, cut incisions in the center of each side. Create a maple leaf shape.

5

すべての辺に切り込みが入った状態。

All the side faces have incisions.

6

葉の一番先からむく。角から丸みを持たせながら切り込みに向かって深めに切る。

Beginning at the top, create a rounded shape towards the depth of the incision just made.

7

1カ所の片側を切った状態。

The round shape is made on one side.

8

中央に切り込みを入れた5辺は、角から切り込みの深いところに向かって、丸みをつけて切る。

In the same manner, create a rounded shape towards the depth of the next incision.

9

片側が1周切れた状態。

Repeat until the same sides are "peeled" slightly rounded.

残り半分も同様に切る。

Work the other way around.

紅葉形にむき終わった状態。

The completed block of maple leaf shape.

端から薄く切る。

Lay on a cutting board, slice thinly.

水にさらしてシャキッとさせる。

Soak in cold water until crisp.

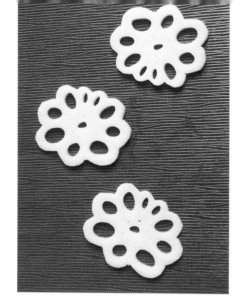

れんこんの穴の形を生かして菊の花に見立てます。
使うれんこんによって表情の違う菊の花ができあが
ります。割れやすいので注意するか、塩水に漬けて
から作業しましょう。

KIKKA RENKON
<ruby>菊花<rt>きっか</rt></ruby>れんこん
Lotus Root Crysanthemums

The chrysanthemum has been used as a noble emblem,
the Imperial crest, so this flower takes on a particular
meaning to the Japanese.
A different expression is created according to the natural
patterns of the root.
Be careful as the root is easily breakable. I recommend
soaking in salted water before peeling.

1

れんこんはむきやすい厚さの輪切り
にし、穴と穴の間に切り込みを入れる。

Cut a manageable thickness of lotus
root. Cut an incision around two holes.

2

切り込みの間から切り込みに向かっ
て、穴の丸みに沿って丸くむく。

Peel along the round holes, in one
direction.

3

片側をむいた状態。

One side is rounded off.

4

同様に反対側も穴に沿ってむく。

In the same manner, peel the other side.

5

穴に沿ってすべてむけた状態。

Both sides are peeled along the holes.

6

厚みは用途に合わせて小口から切る。これは3㎜ほど。

Slice according to the purpose. This is 3mm thick.

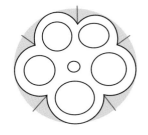

穴と穴の間に切り込みを入れ、その深いところをつなぐように穴の丸みに沿ってむく。

Make incisions between the holes, and peel along the holes, linking the incisions smoothly.

JAKAGO RENKON

蛇籠れんこん
Lotus Root Basket Weave

穴の開いたれんこんを縦方向にむき、その模様を楽
しみます。つなげてむくことで美しい透かしが現れ、あ
しらいとしても華やかで、料理に栄えるむきものです。

In old Japan long bamboo baskets were filled with
gravel and placed on the riverbank to protect. By peeling
lotus root, you can make this interesting strip makes a
surprising dish.

1

れんこんは皮をむき、輪切りにする。
縦にむいていくので、ある程度高さ
があった方がよい。これは8㎝ほど。

Cut lotus root into a long enough block
for the vertical peeling (This piece is
8cm thick). Peel the skin. Start peeling
away the corners.

2

角に包丁を入れ、縦に丸くなるよう
に角をむく。

Make a thick slice at corners to round
up the whole block.

角を落として丸く整えた状態。

Prepared block rounded all around.

薄く桂むき (P.22) をする。

Work thin Katsura-muki (P.22).

厚さを均等にしてつなげてむく。

Continue peeling into even thickness.

れんこんの穴が透かしとなり、美しい模様が連続するむきものとなる。

Let the holes of the root create a stretch of beautiful lacy pattern.

ICHIMONNJI MOROKOSHI

一文字もろこし
いちもんじ

Letter-1 Corn

もろこしを「むく」という、発想がおもしろいむきもの。粒を列にしてむくことで食べやすくなります。食べやすさは、おいしさにつながる大きな要素でもあります。

Corn can be "peeled" into vertical strips, making it easy to eat. Cutting into easy-to-eat sizes and shapes will improve the taste of the food.

1

もろこしを蒸して、熱いうちにラップをきつく巻く。冷めたら取り出し、必要な長さに切る。

Steam corn, and while it is hot, tightly wrap with a plastic wrap. Let cool, unwrap and cut into a length you need.

92

2

長すぎるとむきにくくなり、また崩れやすくなるので、ほどよい長さがよい。

Be sure it is a manageable length. If it is too long, the corn will break easily.

3

粒の並びに沿って包丁を入れ、芯の固いところギリギリをむく。

Insert the knife along the vertical line until reaching the hard core. Peel sideways.

4

1周を何回かに分け、ある程度つなげてむく。

Divide the round into several sections, but continue peeling until a certain width is done.

5

むいたもろこしを使いたい幅に指で割る。

Using your hand, split into required widths.

AOBA TOGAN

青葉冬瓜
Wax Gourd Leaves

冬瓜は、「冬までもつ」ことからその名がつけられた夏
野菜。加熱すると果肉が翡翠色に透き通り、とろり
とした独特の食感になります。煮崩れしやすいため、
大きめに切り、葉脈は三角のみを使って彫ります。

The name "togan" means winter gourd, but it is a
summer vegetable which keeps well into winter. When
cooked, the flesh turns a transparent jade-like color, and
is meltingly smooth. To prevent breakage during the
cooking, cut into a large piece, and carve veins using a
chisel.

1

冬瓜をむきたい青葉の大きさに切る。

Cut wax gourd into a desirable size.

2

内側の三角になっている果肉を切り
落とし、平らにする。煮崩れしやす
いので厚みを持たせておく。

Cut away the center triangle to obtain
a flat face. Leave a certain thickness to
prevent breakage.

3

皮を極薄くむき、表面に青味を残す。

Peel off a thin layer of the skin, but
not completely so that trace of green
remains.

4

葉先になる両角を斜めに落とし、粗
く形作る。

Roughly shape a leaf by trimming
away corners that will become the tip.

5

包丁を一息に動かし、滑らかな葉の
輪郭を整える。

In a smooth, single motion, peel the
side to shape the outline of a leaf.

6

葉の形に整えた状態。葉先を気持ち
上向きにすると表情がつく。

Roughly cut leaf block. Raise the tip of
leaf slightly for a natural impression.

7

すべての角を面取りする。

Round off any corners.

8

三角のみで葉脈を入れる。先に向
かって線が細くなるように力を加減
して彫る。

Using a chisel, carve veins. Adjust
your pressure so that the veins become
thinner toward the tip of leaf.

葉先になる両角を斜めに切り落とし、葉
の形を粗く作っておくと、形を整えると
きにむきやすくなる。

Cut away corners diagonally. Such rough
shaping enables easier peeling for later.

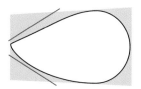

青葉冬瓜 しょうがあんかけ
（あお ば とう がん）
Wax Gourd with Ginger Sauce

青葉冬瓜　エビ　巻きゆば　三度豆　しょうが
Aoba Togan　Prawn　Rolled yuba　Sandomame　Fresh ginger

冬瓜で夏の生き生きと葉を広げる青葉を表現し、食材それぞれを
はっきりと見せることで色合いを際立たせた盛りつけにしました。
しょうがあんでしっとりと食べる、夏の炊き合わせです。

Summer's growing green leaves are set off in combination with
different colors and shapes of food. This summery dish is enhanced
with the thick ginger sauce.

CHASEN KONASU

茶せん小なす
Eggplant Tea Whisk

小なすに切り込みを入れ、油で揚げたあとで皿に押しつけて形作るむきもの。むき方は簡単なものの、品のある存在感でおもてなしにも向きます。切れ目を入れる幅を変えれば、表情も変わります。

Miniature eggplants are scored, deep-fried and squashed onto a plate. It is named after the twisted appearance of the tea whisk used in the Japanese tea ceremony. While easy to create, this mukimono will make an elaborate impression for guests. Change the width of scores for different presentations.

1

なすのへたを切り取る。

Trim away the stem section.

2

切り取りたいところに刃を当て、なすを回して取る。

Apply the knife at a position you want, and make a score all around, turning the eggplant with your left hand.

3

へたが小さく整った状態。

When the stem section has been detached, the eggplant looks like a whisk handle.

4

包丁の刃元を使い、縦に切り込みを入れる。

Using the base of the knife, make a deep vertical incision.

5

適当な幅で1周切り込みを入れる。

Repeat making incisions all around, the same width apart.

6

180℃の油で揚げ、なすの頭を持って、皿に押しつけながらひねり、形作る。

Deep-fry in 180℃；oil heated drain. Place on the serving dish and push down with a twisting motion.

97

加茂なすねじむき
Twist-peeled Eggplant

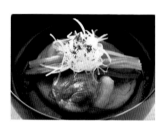

ねじむきは、なすなどの丸いものをむくのに適した手法で、表面積が増えるので、味がよく染み、揚げ物にもむきます。曲線に沿ってむくことができ、ムダがありません。

This is a good peeling method for round shapes such as eggplants, and leaves little waste. By creating more surface area, the vegetables absorb the flavor. Suitable for frying as well.

1

なすはへたを切り落とす。

Trim away the stem part of the eggplant.

2

下部も切り落とし、円柱形にする。

Trim away the bottom to create a cylinder.

98

3

刃元から皮に入れ、なすを外側にね
じりながら包丁を引いてむく。

Insert the base of your knife beneath
the skin of eggplant. Turn the vegetable
away from you as you move the knife
downwards.

4

なすの形に逆らわず、細く細かくむ
いていく。

Peel along the outline of the eggplant,
leaving a very narrow strip of peel.

5

半分ほどむけた状態。

Half of the skin is peeled off.

6

包丁は刃元から刃先までを大きく使
う。

Using the knife from the bottom to top
direction, peel with a drawing motion.

7

包丁は同じリズムで上下に動かし、
なすを回す。

Move the knife in the same rhythm as
you turn the eggplant.

8

なすをねじりながらむくため、ねじ
むきと呼ばれる。

As the name suggests, the streaks are
twisted.

KONOHA KABOCHA

木の葉かぼちゃ
Squash Leaves

葉のギザギザの角度を変えてむくと、それらしい形に。
かぼちゃの黄色が紅葉した葉を思わせます。皮の緑
色を少し残し、紅葉しつつある葉を表現してもおも
しろみがあります。

To make them resemble the shapes found in nature, cut the rugged edges
irregularly. The yellow color reminds you of the autumn leaves.
Peel incompletely leaving a hint of green, which could suggest the colors turning.

1

カーブがちょうどよい、かぼちゃの
上部を使う。かぼちゃは硬いので、
牛刀を使って切るとよい。

Use a top section of squash. This part
has the best curve for this purpose.
Cut hard vegetable like squash with
a cleaver.

2

かぼちゃを必要な大きさに切る。

Cut squash into the size needed.

100

3

皮をむく。完全にむいて黄色を出しても、緑をやや残してもよい。

Peel the skin. Either peel completely or leave some green color.

4

横にしてまな板に置き、内側を切って平らにする。

Place on a cutting board flat side down, and cut away inside to flatten.

5

幅がある側の角を三角に切り、粗い葉っぱの形にする。

Cut away the wider end into a triangle.

6

葉っぱの形に粗くむいた状態。細い方が葉先になる。

Roughly shaped leaf, pointed end being the tip.

7

側面を滑らかな葉の形に切って整える。

Cut the sides in a curve.

8

葉の形をかたどった状態。

Smoothly shaped leaf.

9

側面に切れ目を入れる。

Make incisions into one side of the leaf.

10

切れ目は葉先にいくほど徐々に角度をつけ、深めに入れる。

Make wider and shallower incisions as you work towards the bottom of the leaf.

11

反対側も同様に切れ目を入れる。

Repeat on the other side of the leaf.

12

両側に切れ目が入った状態。

Both sides have incisions.

13

葉先側の切れ目の先から次の切れ目の深いところに向かって、包丁を丸みをつけて切り、葉のギザギザを作る。

Make notches. Begin at the tip and cut into the depth of incision to create a rounded shape.

14

片側をむいた状態。

One side of the leaf is completed.

15

同様に反対側も葉先側の切れ目の先から次の切れ目の深いところに向かって、丸みをつけて切り、葉のギザギザを作る。

In the same manner, make notches with rounded edges on the other side, beginning at the tip.

切り込みは、葉先にいくほど深く、角度をつけて入れ、切り取るときには丸みをつけてむく。

The incisions should become sharper and deeper towards the tip of the leaf.

MATSUTAKE KOIMO

松茸小いも
Taro Mushrooms

小いもの皮をまつたけの笠に見立て、下側を六方に
むいただけの簡単でかわいらしいむきもの。旬の小い
もで秋の味覚を表現した、この時期ならではのあしら
いです。

An easy yet cute mukimono resembling Japanese
treasured mushroom, harvested only in autumn. Using
Roppo peeling method, make an autumnal presentation.

小いもの下部のへたを切り落とす。

Trim away bottom of a small taro.

まつたけの笠を作る。小いもの皮の上から1/4ほどに包丁の刃を当て、小いもを回しながら切れ目を1周入れる。

Make the cap. Insert knife at a quarter length of the taro, and cut deeply turning the taro with your left hand.

下から皮を六方（P.20）にむく。

Peel the skin from the bottom, into Roppo (P.20).

下からむき、切れ目まできたら皮を外す。

Move the knife towards the top, stopping at the deep incision. Remove the thick skin.

菊花京いも
きっ　か　きょう

Kyoto Taro Chrysanthemums

京いもは里いもの一種で、ねっとりとしていて甘みが
あり、煮崩れしにくいので煮物に多く用いられます。
菊の花をデザイン的にとらえた2パターンを紹介し
ます。

Kyo-imo has a subtle sweetness and is popular in
simmered dishes as it retains the shape during the
cooking. I will introduce two patterns for this ingredient.

◆シャープにむく Sharp Edge Chrysanthemum Pattern

1

京いもは太さがそろった真ん中あた
りを輪切りにする。これは2cm厚さ
ほど。

Cut rounds from the straight, center
part of Kyo-imo. This measures 2cm
thick.

2

皮を薄くむいて丸く木取る。

Peel a thin layer of the skin to make a
round shape.

3

断面に包丁で3㎜ほどの切れ目を入
れる。

Across the cut edge, begin making
incisions 3mm deep.

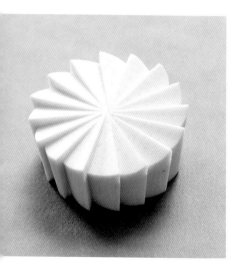

4

まず十字に入れ、その間に 2 本。さらにその間に 4 本。計 8 本の切れ目を入れて、16 等分する。中心がずれないように合わせる。

Cut a crisscross incision. Between two incisions, make 2 incisions only to the center. Repeat with the two incisions, this time making 4 incisions, resulting with 16 incisions at even intervals. Be sure to end at the center point.

5

16 等分した切れ目に合わせ、側面にも縦の切れ目を入れる。同様に深さは 3 mm ほど。

Make 3 mm incisions around the sides, connecting to the top side incisions.

6

ひとつの切れ目から、隣りの切れ目の深いところをつなぐように斜めに切り取る。

Peel away the section between the incisions, cutting towards the depth of the next incision.

7

1 カ所切り取れた状態。

One section is trimmed away.

8

1 周 16 カ所を切り取る。

Repeat until all 16 sections are cut all the way around.

9

中心がずれないように包丁を合わせてむくと、美しく仕上がる。

Try not to displace the center point for a neat finish.

10

側面も同様に、ひとつの切れ目から、隣りの切れ目の深いところをつなぐように斜めに切り取る。

Repeat on the sides, cutting towards the depth of the next incision.

◆丸みをつけてむく Round Edge Chrysanthemum Pattern

1

シャープにむいたパターンと同様に、京いもは丸く木取り、断面に包丁で3mmほどの切れ目を8本入れて16等分する。

In the same manner as Sharp Edge Chrysanthemum, cut out a round from the straight, center part of Kyo-imo. Make 3mm deep incisions into the round top (see step 4, overleaf).

2

切れ目の真ん中から、隣りの切れ目の深いところをつなぐように丸みをつけて切り取る。

Starting from the center of an incision, cut into the depth of the next incision, rounding slightly.

3

1周切り取ったら、反対側からも同様に丸みをつけて切り取る。

When you finish with the original incision, work the other way around, rounding the cut edges.

4

両側から切り取り、丸い花びらにむいた状態。柔らかい印象を与える。

Both sides of the ridges are rounded off, all around.

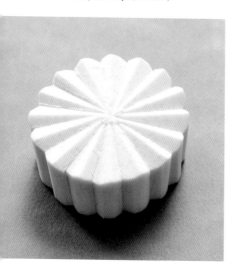

5

側面も同様に、切れ目の真ん中から、隣りの切れ目の深いところをつなぐように丸みをつけて切り取る。

Repeat on the sides, cutting towards the depth of the next incision, rounding the cut edges.

6

側面の片側を丸くむいた状態。

The sides are half done, viewing from the bottom.

7

反対側からも丸く切り取る。

Turn over and repeat on the other side of the ridges.

8

全体に丸みをつけてむき終わった状態。

Both sides of the ridges are rounded off, all around.

同じ菊花にむいた京いもだが、ひと手間加えるだけで見た目の印象が大きく異なる。

Two versions of Chrysanthemum Kyo-imo, giving different impressions.

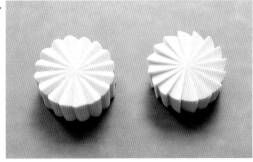

KIKKA KYO-IMO SHIRA-NI
菊花京いも白煮
きっ か きょう　　　しら に
Simmered Taro Chrysanthemums

菊花京いも　菊菜　エビ　菊花
Kikka Kyo-imo　Kikuna greens　Shrimp　Edible Chrysanthemums

京いもは身が締まっていて細かい細工がしやすく、料理の主役となる繊
細な菊の花をむくことができます。煮崩れしにくいので、煮物にぴった
りです。形を見せる盛りつけにし、エビと菊花で色味を添えています。

Kyoi-mo, or Kyoto taro, has a firm texture and is easy to make intricate
carving. These Chrysanthemums can play a principal role on the table. Here
they are displayed simply to show the shapes, accentuated with red shrimp
and chrysanthemums flowers.

菊花小かぶ 海老そぼろがけ

Chrysanthemum Kabu Turnip
with Prawn Sauce

菊花小かぶ　エビ　かぶら菜　菊花　しょうが
Kikka Ko-kabu　Prawns　Turnip greens
Edible chrysanthemum flower　Fresh ginger

シンプルでありながらエビそぼろが色鮮やか
に栄え、中心に据えた白い菊の花を際立たせ
ています。今まさに花を開こうとする、菊の
凛としたたたずまいを皿の上に表現しました。

Simple yet graceful looking white turnip
with thick shrimp sauce drizzled over it. I got
inspired by a dignified appearance of white
chrysanthemums that had just opened.

111

菊花小かぶ
きっ か
Turnip Chrysanthemums

開花前のぽってりとした菊の花を小かぶで表現しま
した。ランダムに入れた花びらの筋が、表情を決める
ポイントです。料理の主役となりうる華と、奥ゆかし
さを兼ね備えたむきものです。

Ready-to-bloom, a plump chrysanthemum bud is created from a small turnip.
Grooves made randomly add expressions. This mukimono possesses
eye-catching yet modest features.

1

葉を切り落とす。

Cut away leaves.

2

六方（P.20）にむく。かぶは皮の内側
に筋があるので、口当たりをよくす
るため、皮を厚くむく。

Peel a thick layer from the turnip to
remove the tough fibers under the skin.
Create the Roppo(P.20) shape.

3 六方にむいた状態。

Roppo shape is completed.

4 六方にむいた角を取り、丸く整える。

Round off any corners to make a smooth surface.

5 丸くぽってりとした形に整えた状態。

Plump, rounded shape of turnip.

6 頂点に包丁をV字に入れ、切り取って筋を入れる。

Into the top of kabu, make "v" scores by inserting knife.

7

中心を合わせ、2本目の筋を1本目
にクロスさせて切り取る。

Adjusting the center point, make
another "v" score at an angle.

8

同様にもう1本入れ、計3本の筋を
切り取る。

Make another "v" score to carve an
asterisk.

9

側面に包丁をV字に入れ、切り取っ
て筋を入れる。頂点に入れた筋の間
に入れていく。

Into the sides of turnip, insert knife
twice to cut a "v" score vertically
between the top scores.

10

さらに、間に包丁をV字に入れ、切
り取って筋を入れる。

Make more "v" scores between the
top scores.

11

斜めの筋や短い筋、長い筋を交え、ランダムに入れる。

Make diagonal, shorter or longer scores randomly.

12

上部を中心に、筋が入った状態。

Top half with "v" scores.

13

上下の位置をずらし、下の方にも包丁をV字に入れ、切り取って筋を入れる。

Turn over the turnip, and repeat scoring in the same manner.

14

かぶ全体に筋が入り、菊の花びらを表現できた。

Completed chrysanthemum bud with scores all over.

KAKUGIRI KABU

角切りかぶ
Offset Turnip Squares

直方体の対角の角を切り落とした形のむきもの
です。直線で作られた形が整然と並ぶ様は美し
く、シンプルでありながら存在感があります。

Offset cube shapes are formed by cutting off a side.
Shapes consisting of linear lines look beautiful when
arranged in a row. This simple mukimono has a great
presence.

1

聖護院かぶは3㎝厚さほどの輪切り
にし、皮をむいて端を切り落とす。

Slice Shogoin Kabu, or large white
turnip, into 3cm thick slices.
Peel and trim away an edge.

2

3〜4㎝ほどの幅に細長く切る。

Cut into 3-4 cm wide columns.

3

端から5mmほどのところに、5mmほどの深さで切れ目を入れる。

Along one long side of the square prism, make 5mm deep incision, 5mm inside the edge.

4

1面左に倒して手前とむこう側をひっくり返し、3と同様に切れ目を入れる。

Turn the prizm left-hand face down. Turn over so the near end becomes farthest. Repeat step 3 to make another incision.

5

角を切り落とした状態。

A thin stick is cut off.

6

角を切り落としたところの対角にある角を同様に切り落とす。

Repeat on the opposite side to cut off edges.

7

ふたつの角を切り落とした状態。

Two opposite corners are cut away.

8

3cmほどの幅で切り分ける。

Cut into 3cm wide cubes.

TAI KABU
鯛かぶ
たい
Sea Bream with Turnips

角切りかぶ　針ゆず　鯛　ほうれんそう
Kakugiri Kabu　Shredded Yuzu　Red Sea Bream　Spinach

鯛とかぶは初冬の出会い物。鯛のアラから出る旨みをたっぷり
吸いこんだかぶは驚くほど柔らか。それでいてかぶはピシッと
角がそろい、美しいまとまりを見せてくれます。

Early winter provides us a harmonious encounter.
Boned red sea bream imparts a rich aroma to turnips, which are
unexpectedly tender, yet the cubes remain their sharp outlines.

SENMEN KABU DENGAKU
扇面かぶ田楽
<ruby>扇面<rt>せんめん</rt></ruby> <ruby>田楽<rt>でんがく</rt></ruby>

Turnip Fan with Sweet Miso

扇面かぶ　エビ　田楽みそ　かぶら菜　ふりゆず
Senmen Kabu　Prawn　Dengaku miso
Turnip greens　Grated yuzu rind

扇は縁起がよいとされ、祝いの料理にも多く用いら
れます。その扇面を聖護院かぶからかたどり、エビ、
かぶら菜、田楽みそで色よく仕上げました。気品あ
るおもてなしの一品です。

Suehiro, or another name of fan, implies a broader
future as it widens upwards, and this shape has been
favored in celebration displays. This fan is made from
Shogoin kabu, and sweet miso sauce drizzles over it.
Prawn and greens add color while yuzu particles are
dispersed to create an elegant appetizer.

扇面かぶ
せ ん め ん

Turnip Fans

晩秋から初冬に甘みを増して旬を迎える聖護院かぶ
を扇面かぶに仕立てました。器や用途に合わせてで
きあがりの大きさをイメージしましょう。

The autumn-into-winter transitional season gives a sweet
flavor to Shogoin kabu, or Kyoto turnip. Estimate the
finished size by the container and purpose.

1

聖護院かぶは2cmほどの厚さの輪切
りにし、皮をむいて半月に切る。そ
こから器や用途に合わせ、作りたい
大きさのいちょう(P.14)に切る。

Cut a 2cm wide slice from the large
turnip. Peel and cut in half. Cut off
Icho(P.14) to required size for the
serving dish and purpose.

2

大きさを決めた状態。

The base of the fan is ready.

3

すべての角を面取り（P.15）する。

Round off any corners (P.15).

4

いちょうの尖っている部分を切り落とし、扇形にする。角を面取りする。

Trim away the pointed corner and round off the sharp corners.

5

上面に均等な切れ目を3㎜ほどの深さに入れる。

Make even scores 3mm deep in a radial fashion.

6

切れ目の本数は大きさによって変え、バランスよく見えるようにする。

Adjust the intervals checking the balance of the whole size.

7

切れ目の頂点から、隣りの切れ目の深いところをつなぐように斜めに切り取る。

Applying the knife along the first score, cut at a slant towards the next score to slice off a narrow triangle.

8

すべて斜めに切り取り、扇の重なりを表現する。

Repeat until you have shaped all the folds of the fan.

KIKKO DAIKON
きっこう
亀甲だいこん
Daikon Tortoise-shells

「亀は万年、鶴は千年」といわれるように、亀は長寿の象徴として縁起がよいとされ、慶事の料理に用いられます。亀の甲羅の模様から、六角形に木取ったものを亀甲と呼びます。

As an old saying goes "Tortoises live 10,000 years, cranes 1,000 years," tortoises are treasured as an emblem of longevity and often used in celebratory dishes. A geometric pattern of hexagons were brought from China in the eighth century, when it was recognized as the shape of tortoise shell. Thus this shape is called Kikko, or tortoise-shell.

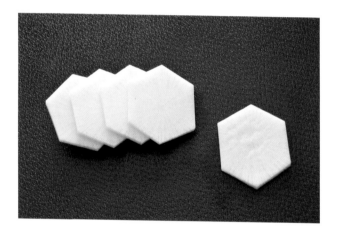

1

だいこんは必要な長さに切る。

Cut daikon into the length you need.

122

2

皮をむいて丸く木取る。

Peel all around.

3

丸く木取っただいこんを六角（P.16）に木取る。

Place on a cutting board and cut away six sides to form a Rokkaku(P.16).

4

六角に木取った状態。

Rokkaku, a hexagonal prism, is completed.

5

用途に合わせた厚さに切る。これは4mmほど。

Slice into required width. This measures 4mm.

SUEHIRO YUZU
末広ゆず
すえひろ
Yuzu Fans

扇のことを末広とも呼び、縁起のよいむきものです。
天に飾り、色味とともに香りを添える吸い口になり
ます。

Since the shape of a fan becomes broader as it goes
farther, it suggests good luck for the future. Yuzu in this
half-folded fan shape adds color and special aroma when
used as a topping for soups.

1

ゆずの側面の皮を幅広くむく。

Peel a wide strip from the sides of
yuzu citron.

2

裏返してまな板に置き、白いわたを
包丁でそぎ取る。

Place on a cutting board white side up,
and slice off the white membrane as it
tastes bitter.

124

3

皮の内側にある白いわたを取り除いた状態。

The white membrane has been removed.

4

端を切り落とし、形を整える。

Trim away the end to make a straight edge.

5

同様に長い部分も端を切り落とし、形を整える。

Trim the longer sides as well.

6

斜めに包丁を入れて三角に切る。包丁をハの字に動かして切ると、上下互い違いに末広ゆずができる。

Cut diagonally into a folding fan shape. Cut into "V" alternating top and bottom.

UME NINJIN

梅にんじん
Plum Blossom Carrots

梅の時期は1月から3月ですが、松竹梅の縁起物
としては1年を通して用いることができます。表
面を斜めにむき取ることで表情がつき、料理に華
を添えます。

Although the season of the Japanese plum is from
January to March, you can use this mukimono all
year round as a good luck symbol. These blossoms
with 3D petals add color and fun.

1

にんじんは必要な長さに切り、皮を
むいて五角（P.18）に木取る。

Cut the length of carrot you need, peel
the skin, and make a pentagon-shaped
block(P.18).

2

すべての辺の中央に深さ3㎜ほどの
切り込みを入れる。

Into the center of each side, make a
3mm-deep incision.

3

角を丸く取りながら切れ目の深いと
ころにむかって丸みをつけて切る。
片側をむいた状態。

Rounding off the corners, make a
round cut into the depth of each
incision. The round petals are made on
one side.

4

同様に反対側も丸みをつけてむく。

In the same manner, work the other way, rounding off the corners.

5

梅の形がむけた状態。

All the petals are rounded off.

6

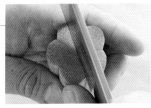

上面の花びらの間に包丁を入れ、中心に向かって切り込みを入れる。計5本入れる。

Insert the knife between the petals on top, and cut an incision towards the center. Make 5 incisions.

7

刃を寝かせて、中心を支点に切れ目から次の切れ目へ斜めに切る。にんじんを回して切る。

Holding the knife, face up along one incision, cut towards the depth of next incision at a slant. Repeat on the next, turning the block.

8

用途に合わせた厚さに切る。これは1cmほど。

Slice to required width. This measures about 1cm.

五角に木取った各辺の中央に切れ目を入れ、角を取るように丸みをつけて切る。

Make deep incisions into the center of each side of the pentagon, then round off the corners.

鶴えびいも
Taro Cranes

羽の中に首をうずめた鶴をくちばしでデザイン的に表現しています。えびいもの細くなっている部分は、料理に合わせて切り落としてもそのまま残しても。

A crane burying its face into its feathers is presented, made from taro. The narrower tip of taro can be cut away or left as it is, depending on the dish.

1

えびいもの上部を切り落とし、五角（P.18）にむく。

Cut away from the wide end of taro, and remove a thick layer of the peel towards the tip to create Gokaku (P.18).

2

五角のまま、えびいもの形に添ってむく。

Peel along the sides of taro to shape a tapered Gokaku.

128

3

包丁は一息に動かしてなめらかなラインを作る。

Move the knife in a single motion to create a smooth face.

4

五角にむいた状態。

Completed Gokaku.

5

辺の中央からひとつ飛ばした辺の中央に切れ目をV字に入れる。

Make a "V" incision from the center of one side towards the opposite side.

6

飛ばした辺から刃を入れ、切れ目の深いところに向かって斜めに切り落とす。

Apply the knife along the adjacent side (right-hand edge) and slice into the depth of the incision just made, at a slant.

7

両側を切り落とす。

Turn around and repeat with the other side.

8

両側を切り落とした状態。

Both sides are trimmed away, leaving the bird's beak.

9

細い部分を適当な長さに切る。そのまま料理に使ってもよい。

Trim away excess of the narrower end, if necessary.

KAME TAKENOKO

亀たけのこ
Bamboo Shoot Tortoises

長寿の象徴で縁起がよいとされる亀の中でも、甲羅に蓑をつけたように藻がついている蓑亀は、特に珍重されるめでたいものです。

Of all the tortoise shells created as lucky symbols, this Minogame has a special feature, the algae stuck on the sides of shell.

1

たけのこの先の部分を使う。大きさによって、半分または1/4に切る。

Use only the small, top part of bamboo shoot. Cut into halves or quarters depending on its size.

2

まな板に置き、六角（亀甲）に切る。

Place on a cutting board, trim into Kikko, or hexagons.

130

3

四方の角を落とすイメージで六角に
整え、つるっとしている部分もあえ
て残す。

A hexagon is made by just cuting off
triangle from each corner. Leave the
shiny top section as a tail.

4

六角に切った状態。正六角形ではな
く、縦長に作った方が亀らしく見える。

A hexagon is made. Elongate to mimic
a tortoise.

5

甲羅の模様を入れる。

Make tortoise shell pattern by cutting
crisscross scores.

6

包丁をV字に入れて2本の筋を入れ
る。

Cut "V" scores so that the pattern will
show up.

7

方向を変え、同様に2本筋を入れる。

Turn the "shell" and cut the same
number of scores.

8

甲羅の模様を入れた状態。煮物にす
るので、リアルにしすぎず、イメー
ジ程度に。

The tortoise pattern is completed. It
does not need to look real since they
are usually used in simmered dishes.

ORE MATSUBA

折れ松葉
Yuzu Pine Needles

ゆずの皮のむきものは数多くありますが、松葉を組んだ形の折れ松葉には存在感があり、煮物や吸い物に添えることで、表情を変えることができます。

There are many varieties of yuzu mukimono among which this crossed pattern is often found added to simmered dishes and soups. It changes the overall impression.

1

ゆずの側面の皮を幅広くむく。

Peel a wide strip from the sides of yuzu citron.

2

裏返してまな板に置き、白いわたを包丁でそぎ取る。

Place on a cutting board white side up, and slice off the white membrane.

3

端を切り落とし、形を整える。

Turn over and trim away narrow edges to straighten.

4

同様に長い部分も端を切り落とし、形を整える。

Trim the long sides as well.

5

上の部分はつなげたまま、2㎜ほど
の幅で切り込みを入れる。

Leaving the top section uncut, make a
long slit 2mm inside.

6

裏返して同様に上の部分はつなげた
まま、2㎜ほどの幅で切り込みを入
れる。

Turn over and repeat, leaving the top
section uncut.

7

2㎜ほどの幅で切り離す。

Cut 2mm inside again, this time cutting
all the way through.

8

両側から切れ目が入った状態。

Each end has a deep slit.

9

切り離さずつながっている部分を両
手でそれぞれ持ち、ひねって切れ端
を上にむける。

Hold the connected ends in each of
your hands.

10

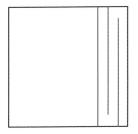

下側の切れ端を上に組ませる。

Twist to bring the lower needle
upwards, and then bring the other
needle over it to cross.

両側から切り込みを入れて切り離す。
同じように切れ目を入れれば、連続
していくつも作ることができる。

Cut deep slits from both ends, and
cut off.
Repeat until you reach the end.

松葉きゅうり
Cucumber Pine Needles

切り離していない部分にのりを巻くと、より松葉らし
い雰囲気が出ます。きゅうりはアレンジの幅が広く、
バリエーションも豊富なので、用途によって使い分
けるとよいでしょう。

Wrap the uncut end with nori seaweed for a realistic
effect. As cucumbers have lots of possibilities as
mukimono, arrange according to the purpose.

1

きゅうりはへたを落とし、作りたい
松葉の長さに切る。

Cut away the stem end. Cut a length
required for the pine needles.

2

皮を厚めにむく。

Peel the skin thickly, into the pine
needle thickness you want.

3

濃い緑の皮だけをむいた状態。

Use only the darker green part.

4

3㎜幅ほどで切れ目を入れ、上部はつなげたままにしておく。

Cut a deep slit 3mm inside, leaving the top uncut.

5

2度目に入れる包丁で切り離す。

Cut at 3mm again, this time all through the length.

6

水にさらしてシャキッとさせ、水気を拭き取ってから、つながっている部分にのりを巻く。

Soak in cold water until crisp. Wipe off moisture with a towel, and wrap a thin piece of nori seaweed around the tops.

1度目に入れた包丁の切れ目は、上部を5㎜ほどつなげたまま残し、2度目の包丁で切り離す。

For the first cut, leave 5mm from the top uncut. Then cut off with the second cut.Repeat alternately.

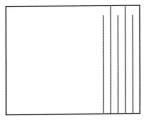

BOTAN DAIKON
牡丹だいこん
Daikon Peony

大ぶりで華やかな初夏の花、白牡丹をだいこんで表現しました。花びらをむきはじめる前の切り込みと丸みを中心がズレないように丁寧にむくことが出来栄えにつながります。

Peony, a magnificent early summer blossom with layers of petals, is depicted in carved white daikon. Work carefully to keep the center point in its position when making incisions all around for a beautiful finish.

1

だいこんを3cmほどの輪切りにし、皮を薄くむいて丸く木取る。

Slice daikon 3cm thick. Remove a thin layer of skin.

2

断面に包丁で3mmほどの切れ目を入れる（図A）。

Into the cut edge, begin making incisions 3mm deep (fig. A).

3

十字に2本、その間に2本の切れ目
が入った状態。

Cut a criss-cross incision. Then make 2
incisions between those just made.

4

切れ目の中央から切り込みの深いと
ころに向かって丸みをつけて切る。

Apply the blade between 2 incisions,
and cut to the depth of the next
incision, rounding the cut surface.

5

片側のみ1周切り終わった状態。

Continue until you reach the beginning.

6

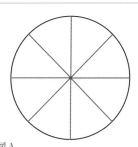

反対側を同様に切り、はじめに入れ
た切れ目に向かって丸い山形になる
ようにする。

Repeat on the other side of the ridge,
rounding each surface.

7

中心を軸に、丸い山形にむいた状態。

Round cut is made around the center
point.

図A
丸く木取っただいこんを8等分する
切れ目を入れる。中心がしっかり合
うようにする。深さは3mmほど。

Fig. A
Make incisions dividing the top of
daikon round into 8 equal sections with
3mm depth. Do not displace the center
point. .

8

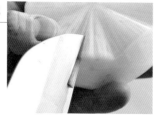

だいこんの中心に刃先を合わせ、山形の左右中ほどに包丁をV字に入れて切り取る（図B）。

Apply the tip of knife to the center point, and cut a shallow "V" on both sides of each mound, and trim away narrow strips (fig.B).

9

山形の左右の丸みにV字の切り込みが入った状態。

The mound has "V" grooves on both sides.

図B
だいこんを横から見た図。山形の頂点を残し、V字に包丁を入れて切り取る。

Fig. B
Side view of the daikon. Leaving the peak of mound, trim away "V" from its sides.

10

1周V字に切り取る。

Repeat all around.

11

牡丹の下となる側の角を1周むく。

Peel the underside of the blossom around.

12

ぽてっとした牡丹のシルエットに整える。

Shape into a plump blossom.

13

外側から中心までつなげて厚めにむく。むきにくいときは塩水に漬けて柔らかくするとむきやすくなる。

Peel the slanted sides all around, into a rather thick strip. If the daikon is brittle, make it supple by soaking in salty water for a while.

14

むいたものをくるくると元に戻し、水にさらしてシャキッとさせる。

Peel into a single strip. Roll the strip into the original shape, and soak in cold water until crisp.

15

めしべとおしべをにんじんでむく。皮をむいて、**14**の牡丹の中心に入るように大きさを合わせ、下が細くなる形に整える。

Make the center of the blossom with carrots. Peel the skin until it fits into the center of petals. Peel a thicker layer towards the bottom.

16

上になる断面（太い方）の角をやや厚めに取る。

Round off the upper edges by peeling a little thicker layer.

17

上の面に包丁を格子状に入れる。

Cut a criss-cross score on the top.

18

牡丹と一緒に水にさらしてシャキッとさせる。

Soak with daikon until crisp.

菊花かぶ
Turnip Chrysanthemums

聖護院かぶを使って作る、小さな菊の花のむき
もの。大きく切るよりも小さめに作った方が食
べやすく、品があります。食感を楽しめる甘酢
漬けがおすすめです。

Fluffy mums are made from a single Shogoin
Turnip. Make them small for an elegant and
modest, and what is more important, they are easy
to eat. I recommend pickling them lightly for a
pleasant texture.

1

聖護院かぶは3cm厚さほどの輪切り
にし、皮をむいて端を切り落とす。

Cut a slice of 3cm thickness from
Shogoin turnip. Peel the skin and cut
away one side and its opposite side.

2

下1/3ほどは切り離さないようにし
て、細かい切り込みを入れる。

Make deep incisions to two thirds of
the thickness, as narrow as possible.

3

切り込みが入った状態。

Deep incisions are made vertically.

4

かぶを90°回転させて端を落とし、同様に細かい切り込みを入れる。

Turn 90º and make cuts in the same manner.

5

縦横に切り込みが入った状態。

Incisions are made vertically and horizontally.

6

3cm幅の棒状に切り、90°回転させてまた3cm幅に切る。

Cut into 3cm wide sticks. Turn 90º and cut 3cm width.

7

3cm角に切り分けた状態。

3cm cubes are made.

8

塩水に漬けてしんなりさせてから、甘酢に漬け、盛りつけの際に箸で開いて中心に赤唐辛子の輪切りをのせる。

Soak in salted water until supple. Drain and squeeze. Marinate in a sweet vinegar. Lightly squeeze and fluff the narrow petals. Top with a slice of red chili pepper.

KIKKA DAIKON

菊花だいこん
Daikon Chrysanthemums

桂むきにしただいこんに切れ目を入れ、巻いて菊の花びらを表現します。めしべとおしべはにんじんでむき、組み合わせました。水にさらしてシャキッとさせ、大輪が開く様は見事です。

This mukimono is easier than you would think. Peel daikon into Katsura-muki sheets, cut slits, and roll. The center of flower is made of carrot. The petals "blooms" by soaking in cold water.

1

だいこんは10cm長さのものを40cmほど桂むき（P.22）にし、塩水に5分ほど漬けてしんなりさせる。

Cut daikon into 10cm length. Make Katsura-muki(P.22) and soak in salty water until supple.

2

しっかり水気をきっただいこんをまな板に広げ、縦半分にふんわりとたたむ。

Drain well and spread on a cutting board. Gently fold lengthwise in half, away from you.

3

端から5mmほどの間隔で切れ目を入れる。はじめは小さな切れ目にし、徐々に大きな切れ目にする（図）。

From one side, make deep slits at 5mm intervals, gradually deepening the cut(fig.).

4

めしべとおしべになる部分をむく。にんじんの細い部分を使い、半分にたたんだだいこんよりやや短いくらいの長さに切る。

Make the center. Cut thin part of carrot into a length slightly shorter than the folded daikon sheet.

142

5

にんじんの太い方を面取りの要領で
丸く整える。

Round off the edges of the thicker end.

6

にんじんの上面にV字に包丁を入れ
て、格子状のラインを入れる。

Make criss-cross scores on the beveled
end, by making "V" cuts in both
directions.

7

3のだいこんを切れ目が浅く、たた
んだ輪が上になるようにして広げ、
6のにんじんをのせ、くるくると巻く。

Place the carrot center on the edge of
the daikon sheet, the folded side away
from you. Roll up.

8

巻き終わりに爪楊枝を刺して止める。

Secure the end piercing with a
toothpick.

9

水にさらし、塩分を抜くと、花びら
1枚1枚がシャキッとし、花のよう
に広がる。

Soak in cold water to remove salt. The
petals will become crisp and open like
a flower.

切れ目をはじめは浅く、だんだん深
くしていく。巻いたときに外にいく
につれ広がり美しく仕上がる。

Make the slit deeper as you cut towards
the end. Roll up with the beginning,
and the outer petals will spread
beautifully.

TSUBAKI NINJIN
椿にんじん
<small>つばき</small>
Carrot Camellias

パーツごとにむき、楊枝でつなげて完成させます。料理の一部としてきたむきものとは少し異なりますが、バリエーションのひとつとして紹介します。

Each part is cut out separately and assembled with a toothpick.This mukimono is simply used as a display, different from the others.

◆花びらを作る Make Petals ─────────

1

にんじんは必要な長さに切って皮をむき、丸く木取ったのち、六角 (P.16) に木取る。

Cut a required length of carrot. Make Rokkaku(P.16).

2

六角に木取った状態。

Rokkaku, or hexagonal prism is completed.

3

椿の花びら1枚をイメージしながら、花びらの形に輪郭を整える（図）。

Imagining the shape of a petal, trim the contour of carrot (fig.).

4

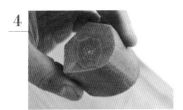

片側を花びら形に整えた状態。

One side of the petal is done.

5

両側をむいて花びら形に整えた状態。

Trim the other side for a completed petal.

6

花びらを横方向に下からカーブをつけて切る。

Holding the column pointed edge down, "peel" from a side.

7

花びらは、花一輪につき5枚作る。

Make 5 petals per blossom.

にんじんを六角に木取り、その中に花びらの形をかたどる。椿の花びらはふっくらとした丸形に。

Shape carrot into a hexagonal column, and cut into a wide, camellia petal.

次のページにつづく▶
To be continued on the next page

◆めしべとおしべを作る　Make Center

8

長さ2cmほどのだいこんを細くむいて整え、椿の中心に収まるくらいの大きさにする。余った部分などを使うとよい。

Cut out a 2cm length of daikon, or use a remnant. Trim into a small cylinder to fit into the blossom.

9

花びらの大きさに合わせて作る。これは長さ2cm、直径1.5cmほど。

Adjust the size to carrot petals. This measures 2cm long, 1.5cm in diameter.

11

ペティナイフで側面から切れ目を入れ、つながっている中だけを切る。

Using a petty knife, cut a into the sides where the corer reached, and cut only the center cylinder.

10

ひとまわり小さい筒抜きを刺し、完全に抜かずに下を3mmほどつなげておく。

Choose a Tsutsu-nuki or corer slightly smaller than the cylinder, and insert into the daikon, leaving 3mm from the bottom uncut. Remove the corer.

12

中だけが抜ける。抜いたものもとっておく。

Remove the inner cylinder. Keep both for later.

◆がくを作る　Make Calyx

13

きゅうりの細い部分を3cmほど使う。

Cut out a 3cm length from thinner part of cucumber.

146

14

皮の内側にペティナイフをさし、刃先で円錐状に切り取る。

Insert the tip of petty knife into the inside of the cucumber skin, and cut away a small cone turning the cucumber around.

15

切った部分を外す。

Remove the cone.

◆組み立てる Assemble

16

5枚の花びらを重ね、円錐状に切ったきゅうりに合わせて爪楊枝を上から刺して止める。

Layer 5 petals and using a toothpick secure the pointed bottoms into the hollow of cucumber, at the center.

17

爪楊枝を軸に、花びらをゆっくり広げる。爪楊枝は押し込むか、飛び出している部分を少し残して切る。

Gently slide each petal around the toothpick. When all the petals are spread, push the toothpick inside or cut away excess, leaving the top to stick out.

18

だいこんの外側を椿の真ん中の爪楊枝に刺す。切った部分を外す。

Set the daikon tube onto the center toothpick.

19

抜いてあっただいこんを戻し、飛び出している楊枝に軽く刺す。

Put back the center cylinder and set onto the toothpick.

TSUBAKI MORI
つばき
椿盛り
Sashimi Camellias

椿にんじん　マグロ　イカ　イクラ　炒り玉
Tsubaki Ninjin　Tuna　Squid　Ikura　Iri Tama

厳しい冬を耐えしのび、花を咲かせる椿と、花びらに舞い落ちる白い雪。静かな冬の情景を造りで表現しました。マグロ、イカ、イクラを椿のつぼみに仕立て、葛の雪を降らせて椿にんじんとマッチさせました。

A wintertime presentation with carrot camellias and sashimi camellia buds, with a hint of snow.

フルーツのむきもの

FRUIT MUKIMONO

フルーツはそのまま食べるものなので、野菜とはまた違ったむき方があります。楽しく豪華な演出に散りばめられた、食べやすさを考えたむきもののアイデアも必見です。

Fruits are served raw as desserts in Japan, and there are different cutting methods than those for vegetables. Check out the ideas hidden under pleasant display.

結びレモン

Knotted Lemon Slices

レモンの皮を切って端をつなげておき、結んであしらいのアクセントにします。料理に黄色の色味を加え、さっぱりさせる添え物のレモンも、ひと工夫を加えることで動きが出て華やかさが増します。

Lemon peel is tied into a decorative knot at the end of a slice. Lemon enhances the dish with its yellow color and refreshing flavor, and a little twist will add a movement and a festive touch.

1

レモンの両端を切り落とす。

Trim away both ends of the lemon.

2

縦半分に切る。

Cut lengthwise into halves.

3

5㎜厚さの半月に切る。

Cut into 5mm thick slices.

4

半月に切ったレモンの皮と果肉の間に包丁を入れて固定し、まな板の上を転がすようにレモンを動かして切る。

Hold a slice on a cutting board as shown, insert the tip of knife between the rind and flesh. Separate the peel by "rolling" the lemon slice.

5

皮はすべて切り落とさず、5㎜ほどつながったままになるところで止めておく。

Do not cut through, and leave 5mm end uncut.

6

皮と果肉が切り離され、わずかにつながっている状態。

Lemon rind and flesh are scarcely joined at an edge.

7

切れている皮で輪を作る。

Make a circle with the separated rind.

8

輪に皮を通して結ぶ。

Bring the end into the loop and tie into a single knot.

いちご

Strawberries

切れ目を入れて花のように開き、丸くくり抜いたキ
ウイフルーツを入れます。赤と緑のコントラストが美
しく、かわいらしい一品です。

Shiny red "buds" hold green centers to make a charming
dessert. Deep-cut strawberry is opened from the bottom
to hold the kiwi balls.

1

いちごは半分に切り込みを入れる。

Cut strawberry from the end deeply
just reaching the calyx.

2

十字に切り込みを入れ、へた部分は
つなげておく。

Make criss-cross cut deeply, but do not
cut the calyx.

3

切れ目を開いた状態。

Gently open the "petals."

4

いちごの切れ目に入る大きさのいも
抜きを選び、キウイフルーツを丸く
ぬく。

Using a melon baller which scoops
small enough balls to set in the
strawberry, and scoop out kiwi.

5

キウイフルーツを箸でいちごに入れ
る。

Set the kiwi ball in the "petals."

153

りんご
Apples

切り分けて芯を取り除き、元の形に戻しています。皮を市松模様にむき、おしゃれに仕上げました。りんごは色が変わりやすいので塩水に浸して色止めしましょう。

Apples are cut into wedges and reassembled after removing the core, creating a checkered pattern. Prevent peeled sections from discoloring by soaking in salted water.

1

りんごの底を薄く切り、座りをよくする。

Slice off the bottom of apple thinly to let the fruit sit.

2

底を切り離す。

Cut a thick slice from the cut bottom.

3

ペティナイフで中央に1周切れ目を
入れる。

Using the petty knife, cut a horizontal
score all around the center (of the
original apple).

4

半分に切る。

Cut in half vertically.

5

ラインをそろえるため、丸のまま8
等分にする。

Holding the apple, cut into eight
wedges aligning the cut across the
center.

6

縦に8等分した状態。

8 equal wedges are made.

7

皮を上半分むく。次は下半分をむき、
元に戻したときに市松模様になるよ
うにする。

Using the center score, peel the upper
skin of a wedge.

8

芯を取り除く

Cut away the core.

9

底を置いて、元の形に戻す。

Peel the adjacent wedge only on the
bottom half. Alternate peeling section
to create a checkered pattern. Set on
the bottom slice to regain the original
shape.

10

塩水に軽く浸し、色止めをする。

Dip in salted water briefly to prevent
discoloring.

マンゴー

Mango

マンゴーの皮を中央だけつなげてむき、結んで持ち手
にしました。手で持って食べられるむきものです。

Mango skin is peeled from both ends to retain the center
section, and tied into a knot, which can be used as a
handle when eaten.

1

マンゴーは真ん中の種を避け、片側
の果肉を切る。

Avoiding the stone, slice one side of
the mango.

2

食べやすい大きさに切る。

Cut into easy-to-eat slices.

156

3

ペティナイフで皮を両側から切り、
中央はつなげておく。

Using the tip of the petty knife, peel
from the end and stop near the center.
Repeat on the other end.

4

ペティナイフの刃先を皮と果肉の
間に入れ、果肉を動かしてむく。

Apply the knife between the skin and
fruit, and move the fruit to peel.

5

皮を中央で結ぶ。

Bring the strips of peel over to the
center, and tie into a knot.

6

皮を結び、持ち手を作った状態。**1**
で切り離した種の上に盛りつける。

The knot serves as a handle to hold.
Arrange on the mango remaining from
step **1**.

オレンジ

Orange

皮をらせん状にむいて果肉を取り出し、食べやすく切り分けて元に戻しました。くるくるとしたラインがデザイン的でおもしろみがあります。

This orange is peeled in a spiral and put back to the original shape after slicing the fruit. Fun design to look at.

1

オレンジは底を薄く切り落とし、座りをよくしてからやや厚めに切る。

Slice off the bottom of orange thinly to let the fruit sit.

2

へた部分にペティナイフを入れ、切り離さずにつなげておく。

Insert the petty knife below the stem, and slice almost through,but not completely.

158

3

ペティナイフを一度外し、皮がくっついている部分から入れる。

Remove the knife and insert into the other side.

4

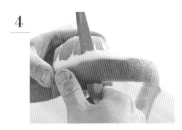

らせん状に皮をむき、底はつなげたまま厚めに切る。

Peel into a curly strip, and stop at the bottom section.

5

筒抜きで真ん中の白いわたを抜く。

Using a corer, remove the center membrane.

6

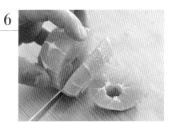

食べやすいよう、輪切りにする。

Slice into easy-to-eat rounds.

7

皮の両側を面取り（P.15）し、外側に白いラインが見えるようにする。

Work Mentori (P.15) along the strip of peel so as to show the white spiral.

8

三角のみでへた部分にも白いラインをつなげて入れる。

Using a corner chisel, make a decorative score to continue upwards.

9

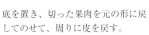

底を置き、切った果肉を元の形に戻してのせて、周りに皮を戻す。

Place the bottom piece. Assemble the cut pieces of orange on it, and wrap with the spiral peel.

島谷宗宏（しまたに　むねひろ)

1972年奈良県生まれ。高校卒業後、「京都新都ホテル松浜」にて、黒崎嘉雄氏に師事する。その後「嵐山辨慶」「貴船ひろや」等で修業を積み、「都旬膳　月の舟」の料理長を経て、2012年「宮川町　水簾」料理長に就任。2009年には、日本料理アカデミー「第2回　日本料理コンペティション」において、近畿・中国・四国地区予選大会で優勝。2010年テレビ東京TVチャンピオンR「世界包丁細工王決戦」でチャンピオンになる。その美しい包丁技は著書『日本料理　最新むきもののワザ』で堪能できる。その他、著書『季節の椀もの入門』『一度は作ってみたい　極みの京料理50』がある。

Munehiro Shimatani

was born in 1972 in Nara, an ancient capital of Japan, and right after graduating high school he began his apprenticeship under Yoshio Kurosaki, one of the top chefs at Kyoto Shinto Hotel Matsuhama. He continued his study in Kyoto restaurants such as Arashiyama Benkei, and Kihune Hiroya before he was appointed chef at Miyako-Shun-Zen Tsuki-no-Fune, Nara's traditional restaurant. Since 2012 he has been serving as Head Chef at Miyagawa-cho Suiren, Kyoto. Munehiro won the semi-finals at "The Second Japanese Culinary Art Competition" held by The Japanese Culinary Academy in 2009. The next year, he became Champion of "World Food Carving" broadcast by TV Tokyo nationwide. His splendid knife techniques are unveiled in this book. His other publications include "Seasonal Soups for Beginners" and "50 Ultimate Kyoto Dishes You Wanted to Cook at Least Once."

協力／宮川町　水簾
京都市東山区宮川筋2-253
TEL 075-748-1988
http://www.kyoto-suiren.com

Staff
撮影／Photo　岩崎奈々子
装丁・デザイン／Design　菊池加奈
文／Writer　木村亜紀子
編集／Editor　植田晴美・水谷和生
翻訳／Translator　石黒陽子

Japanese-English Bilingual Books
四季折々の料理を彩る野菜の飾り切り
英語訳付き　日本料理
むきものハンドブック
Handbook on Japanese Food:
Carving Techniques for Seasonal Vegetables
NDC 596

2015年6月12日　発　行

著　者　島谷　宗宏（しまたに　むねひろ)
発行者　小川雄一
発行所　株式会社 誠文堂新光社
〒113-0033　東京都文京区本郷3-3-11
編集 TEL 03-5800-7762
販売 TEL 03-5800-5780
http://www.seibundo-shinkosha.net/
印刷所　株式会社　大熊整美堂
製本所　和光堂　株式会社